A guide to the markets of Britain

In the same series

A guide to the markets of Britain

Linda Sonntag

Constable London

First published in Great Britain 1988
by Constable and Company Limited
10 Orange Street, London WC2H 7EG
Copyright © 1988 by Linda Sonntag
Set in Linotron Times 9 pt by
Rowland Phototypesetting Limited
Bury St Edmunds, Suffolk
Printed in Great Britain by
The Bath Press Limited, Avon

British Library CIP data
Sonntag, Linda, *1950–*
A guide to the markets of Britain.
1. Great Britain. Markets. Visitors' guides
I. Title
381'.18'0941

ISBN 0 09 466800 0

Contents

Acknowledgements

Nearly four hundred people in Tourist Information offices, public libraries, town halls and in markets have helped me with information for this book. If I have left anything out or made any mistakes, I hope they will get in touch and tell me so. I should like to thank everyone who wrote to me.

L.S.
1987

Introduction

Markets and fairs used to be pretty much the same thing. The word 'fair' comes from the Latin *feria*, feast day, and 'market' from *mercatus*, trade, and from the Old English *mark*, meeting-place. In the Middle Ages, when life revolved around religious events, fairs were held after church on the feast day of that church's patron saint. Traders set up stalls in the churchyard, in the church porch and sometimes even in the church itself, certain of attracting a good number of worshippers in a festive mood. The clergy benefited by levying a toll from each of the stallholders.

As these gatherings grew in size they spilled over the churchyard into the town, and settled usually at a place where roads bringing traders and customers converged – this became the market-place. Often a cross was erected there. It served as a reminder of the market's origins, and to seal a bargain with a handshake by the market cross was as good as taking an oath. If you broke your oath, the worst was likely to happen. One panel on the market cross in Devizes tells the story of Ruth Pierce, a market woman who dropped dead after telling a lie. The cross was a landmark and a meeting point for women traders in particular – farmers' wives would gather on benches placed around it to sell butter, eggs and poultry.

In Bristol transactions were concluded not by the cross but outside the Exchange Hall where there are four bronze pillars on the pavement called The Nails. A deal made here gave rise to the saying 'paying on the nail'. 'Tawdry' is another expression connected with markets. It is a shortened version of 'St Audrey', and appeared in the vocabulary wherever a market or fair was held in St Audrey's churchyard offering indifferent goods for sale.

The rights to hold a weekly market were granted in perpetuity by a charter of the monarch to the Lord of the Manor, who collected the tolls – stallage for the stalls, and piccage if the ground had to be broken up with a pick before they were erected. Gates and shire tolls were still in force in Carlisle as late as 1949, when modern transport finally defeated their collection. A bell was rung to open the market. This practice aimed to stop 'forestallers', people who made unfair bargains before trading had begun. Because of the transient nature of markets, they tended to attract unscrupulous characters, and independent courts, called Pie Powder Courts, were set up to deal with offenders on the spot. 'Pie powder' comes from the French *pieds poudreux*, dusty feet – a condition shared by most who had tramped long distances to get there. If found guilty of giving short weight or otherwise cheating the trader could be fined, the day's fines being divided among the town's poor, or he could be punished in the stocks, or worse. In Alnwick today a mock Pie Powder Court is held and 'offenders' are threatened with the ducking chair.

The market place was often the site of civic punishment. In 1436 on King's Lynn's Tuesday Market Place, forty-three women were burned at the stake for witchcraft, a maidservant was burned to death for the murder of her mistress and sixty-three people were hanged for stealing. There was a whipping-post at which children were whipped for disobedience, and the stocks were used for anyone who disturbed the king's peace.

Many of Britain's market towns owe their present layout to the way the streets developed round the markets of the Middle Ages. In the market-place quite often stallholders would succeed in establishing for themselves a permanent site. Wooden stalls turned into shops made of brick and stone. Street names show that traders in the same kind of merchandise grouped together in one area. The Shambles was once the meat market (today a 'shambles' is still a scene of great destruction and wreckage). Other examples are Horsemarket Street, Buttermarket Street, Pig Hill, Knifesmith Gate, Hog Lane and many more. One branch of trade that does not seem to be commemorated in a street name is the slave trade – both male and female slaves were sold in Britain until the fourteenth century, and wife-selling went on for a long time after that. In 1806 George Gowthorpe of Patrington, a village about fifteen miles east of Hull, took his wife to market in a halter and sold her to a Mr Houseman for twenty guineas. In 1851 and again in 1854 wives were sold at Knighton market – each one went for only a shilling.

Farmers would drive their carts to market, often lining them up in the main street and leaving the selling to other members of the family while they took the horses for a drink at the pond, then stabled them behind the pub and installed themselves in the bar. This is the reason why there are so many inns in market towns. Farmers without carts would take their goods to market in panniers strapped to their horses: quite a few of today's British markets are still called pannier markets. Many other goods were on sale apart from farm produce. Markets drew cocklewomen, ropemakers, tin-men and clogmakers. In 1770 Warrington market was praised for its huge variety of fish – it is amazing what came out of the Mersey and the sea just beyond at that time: lampreys, sturgeon, greenbacks, mullet, eels, lobsters, shrimp, prawns and the best and largest cockles in all England.

Until recently, markets were never hygienic places. In 1820 tar barrels had to be burned in Exeter pork market to purify the air. During a plague in 1665 traders from out of town chewed tobacco to ward off the germs and customers had to put the right money in vessels filled with vinegar. The customer was not allowed to examine the goods before purchasing them, and the trader could not check his money. It was of necessity a rare time of trust between the two parties. The plague was responsible for the founding of Newmarket. The disease had spread and forced Exning market to move to a new site – this became Newmarket.

Fairs were gala markets, and they were also granted by charter. Apart from the usual traders they drew itinerant entertainers and sellers of snacks who could be sure to cash in on the holiday mood. There were pedlars, piemen, jugglers, clowns, acrobats, prize fighters, wandering preachers (John Wesley preached in Stroud market, standing on a butcher's block), travelling shows, bull-baiting and menageries. Posters in the town warned people against pickpockets and forbade the use of confetti and teasers, a sort of wire brush used for tickling. Usually a fair was opened with some sort of official ceremony, and in some towns the same ceremony opens today's fairs. In Alnwick there is the Watch and Ward ceremony: the bailiff, constable and other officials drink quantities of wine and strong ale, then march to the market cross where the bailiff proclaims the fair open. The ceremony is sealed with further deep draughts of ale. Barnstaple Fair is declared open when a glove garlanded in flowers is extended from the window of the Guildhall in welcome.

Some fairs were hiring fairs or Mops, at which agricultural workers and domestics would gather and offer themselves for employment. When hired, labourers would decorate their hats with ribbons. A week after the hiring fair was the Runaway Mop, at which employees who felt they had made a bad bargain could change their minds and make new contracts.

Today's markets and fairs are every bit as lively as they were in the past. Modern fairs offer steam rallies, raft races, bed races, barrel-rolling, fire-eaters, unicyclists, tea-dancing, strong men, racing tipsters, motor-cycle stunts, sky-diving, helicopter displays, grass-track racing, escapologists, daredevil artists, Morris men, clog-dancers, pie-eating contests, tugs-of-war, fortune-tellers and brass bands, besides fireworks and funfairs.

Markets nowadays sell everything from double-glazing to silk-flower arrangements. Out-of-the-way places often sell unusual specialities, and it is worth knowing where to look for anchors, pork pies, basket-work, laver bread, pease-pudding, shellfish cooked on request, hand-made lace, ironwork, gingerbread made to a recipe dating from the time of the Crusades, pottery, samphire, chitterlings, black pudding, tapestry work, personality analysis, faggots and peas, cockles, homeopathic remedies, wigs, shortbread, saddlery and natural British wools, pure to breed. Hence this book. Collectors will want to know where they are likely to find bargains. There are regular auctions of antiques, furniture and farm produce all over the country.

Many towns also have special markets and fairs, and unusual customs that have survived through the centuries. Appleby has a famous horse fair; Lincoln has a German Christmas market with trees, carols and *glühwein*; Newcastle has a traditional holiday market with choirs, bands and folk dancing; Bletchley has the peculiar ceremony of the Fenny Poppers; Corby has a Highland Gathering, an unexpected event for a Northamptonshire town; High Wycombe has a mayor-weighing ceremony; and at Honiton the Town Crier throws hot pennies to the assembled children. Many places have Victorian market extravaganzas once a year. In some market towns the pubs are open all day on market day – most have a favourite eating-place which can be recommended to market-goers.

Today's markets are more diverse in style than they ever were – from giants like Birmingham's Bull Ring to treasures like the Horsham market run by Mrs Durrant's family in her back garden. All are full of characters shouting about themselves and their wares as they always have done. In Kettering the florist who stands at the front of the market claims his family has traded there for 300 years without a break. In Gravesend Syd Strong is a popular attraction – he is well known for tossing dinner services into the air and catching them without breakage. It is probably people like these, even more than the bargains they offer, that make markets irresistible and market shopping the most enjoyable kind of shopping there is.

It is always worth visiting a town on its market day if you want to discover the true character of a place. It will give you a chance to talk to the locals as well as hunt out bargains and specialities, and you can follow up an enjoyable morning's browsing with lunch in a nearby pub.

This book gives all the information the market shopper will need, including suggested eating places; and, for convenience, the markets are arranged in alphabetical order.

The markets

Aberdeen
Where: The Green
When: Friday, Saturday
What: a general market, with 27 stalls

Abergavenny (Gwent)
Where: Town Hall building
When: Tuesday, two outdoor sections and one indoor (200 stalls);
Friday, indoor only
What: fish, fruit, vegetables, materials, household goods, bulbs,
army and navy, crockery

A general market for fish, poultry, vegetables and other farm
products existed on the site of the present market hall for many
years prior to the passing of an Act in 1854 which ensured its
continuance, with power to open on Tuesdays and Fridays.

Abergavenny is a prosperous farming centre with one of the
largest cattle markets in South Wales, held every Tuesday. There
are cattle sales on the first and third Friday of each month and a
pony sale on the second Saturday in the month. Large fairs are held
in May and September. The George Hotel in Cross Street is
recommended for lunch.

Abingdon (Oxfordshire)
Where: Market Place
When: Monday
What: local produce, provisions, plants, clothing, bric-à-brac

Until recently the Market Place was known as The Bury – the burgh
or centre of the borough, where in former times the King's officials
kept order. The Market House stood on the site of the present
County Hall as long ago as 1327, when the 'New House' was burned
down during rioting against the Abbey. The name 'New' implies the
existence of an even earlier building. The Abbey was founded in the
seventh century and the first mention of the town is in the

Domesday Book, which refers to it as a market in front of the
Abbey gates: 'ten traders before the gates of the Church'. The
market has been held in the same place, on a Monday, for well over
800 years. There is a three-day Michaelmas Fair in October which
dates back to the Black Death in 1348–9. The fair remained in part a
hiring fair until the end of last century. The small one-day fair a
week later is still called the Runaway Fair, because it provided
employees with a chance to change their minds (see page 12). The
King's Head, East Street, and the Bell, St Helen's Street, are
among good pubs for lunch.

Airdrie (Strathclyde)
Where: Louden Street
When: Tuesday, Friday
What: food, clothing, plants, household goods, fabrics, pet foods

Very good pub lunches are available at the Tudor Hotel, the
Staging Post and JT's Lounge.

Alfreton (Derbyshire)
Where: Institute Lane, town centre
When: Monday, Tuesday, Thursday, Friday, Saturday
What: a variety of food and general retail goods

There are two fairs a year on Alfreton Welfare, one in spring, the
other in autumn. Alfreton's right to hold fairs dates from the
thirteenth century.

Alnwick (Northumberland)
Where: Market Place
When: Saturday
What: fruit, vegetables, bedding, clothes, fancy goods, sweets,
meat, shoes, basketware, hats, bags

A charter granted to Bishop Bec by Edward I in 1297 allowed a weekly market on Saturday and a fair on St Patrick's Eve, though it is certain that there was a market in Alnwick before that date. A Wednesday market and further fairs were granted by Henry VI, but these have long been discontinued. March and November hiring fairs were held for the recruitment of farm workers who gathered outside the Queen's Head Hotel to offer themselves to prospective employers. The early fairs were ushered in with feudal ceremonies, among them the custom of 'Watch and Ward' which is still practised today. This involves the tradesmen of the town getting together with the bailiff, constable and other officials and drinking quantities of wine and strong ale, after which they march to the market cross, where the bailiff proclaims the fair open and the ceremony is sealed with further 'deep draughts of strong Northumbrian ale drunk from silver flagons'. The lordly owner of the fair and market could once try offenders on the spot. The chief offenders were travellers, whose dusty feet gave their name to the 'Pie Powder Court' (see page 10). Mock Pie Powder Courts are held today; the locals attend these ceremonies dressed in costumes of the 1750s. Alnwick fair starts on the last Sunday in June.

Recommended for lunch are the Market Hotel and Nag's Head Hotel in Temple Street, and the Fleece Inn and Plough Inn, Bondgate Without.

Alton (Hampshire)
Where: Market Square
When: Tuesday
What: greengrocery, materials, clothes, household goods, jewellery, garden plants and equipment, sweets, toys, fish, bacon, eggs

A small area of the Market Square is reserved for the deadstock market. At about 1 p.m. there is a sale in the auction mart, when the auctioneer extols the virtues of bedding-plants, flowers, marrows or pheasants, according to season. Every other Friday he holds a furniture auction. Prospective buyers come early to browse with the aid of a catalogue. The Wheatsheaf in Adlams and Market Hotel in the Square are open for lunch or coffee – then it's back to the auction to make a bid.

Ampthill (Bedfordshire)
Where: Market Square
When: Thursday
What: clothes, fish, vegetables, fruit, toiletries, haberdashery

Ampthill (or Ant-Hill) was a prosperous community from the thirteenth century, with a market established as early as 1242. The Market Square is the hub of the town today, as it was in the Middle Ages. It was originally ringed by public houses and coaching inns, the finest survivor being the White Hart, with its Georgian frontage and seventeenth-century murals inside. A covered arcade of shops on the north side of the square dates from 1780, and the Ampthill News Office is the best Georgian shop-front in town – its unique interior with Georgian furnishings is well worth a visit. In the King's Arms Yard, through the half-timbered archway on the south side, you can see ancient buildings with plaster fleurs de lis on their walls and the date 1677. Market day is Thursday, as it was from the first, and traders set up their stalls round the town pump, a Portland Stone obelisk presented to the town by Lord Ossory in 1785.

Recommended for lunch is the Queen's Head in Woburn Street.

Andover (Hampshire)
Where: High Street
When: Thursday, Saturday
What: thirty pitches selling a general range of goods

Andover has a fair in June or July every year. The Weyhill Market three miles away is considered to be that described in the first pages of Thomas Hardy's *The Mayor of Casterbridge*. The Andover market has a refreshment van on site, and there are plenty of pubs down the High Street.

Appleby (Cumbria)
Where: Main Street, Boroughgate
When: Thursday, Saturday
What: a variety of goods with an excellent range of local produce

Appleby is famous for its Horse Fair which is always held on the
second Wednesday in June, though the events that surround the fair
go on for several days and accommodation in the area must be
booked well in advance to avoid disappointment. The travelling
people and horse-traders arrive about a week before the event and
camp out on Fair Hill (formerly Gallows Hill). The town is
completely transformed, some would say taken over, by gypsies,
tinkers and traders of all kinds. Some hoteliers shut up shop
altogether, other establishments welcome the extra business and
stay open at all hours. Visitors come to admire the gypsy vados
(horse-drawn vans) and the luxurious mobile homes drawn by
Range Rovers and Rolls-Royces. Some of the attractions the
travellers bring with them are fortune-telling, children selling lucky
charms, camp-fires in the evening and traditional gypsy music, as
well as disco music blaring from cassette players. The horse-traders
wash their horses in the River Eden at the bridge in the town centre,
and stake them out along the road for several miles around Fair
Hill. On the Tuesday before the official sale (trading actually goes
on all week), there is harness-racing on Holme Farm Field, five
minutes from the town centre. On the Wednesday saddlery and
carriages are sold as well as horses, and a great deal of
merry-making and celebration follows.
   Some say that the fair has been held since the time of James II, by
a charter of 1685 which granted permission 'for purchase and sale of
all manner of goods, cattle, horses, mares and geldings'. Others say
that this fair fell into disuse, and the present June fair has its origins
in the 'New Fair' which was instituted in 1750 as 'a shew of horses
and sheep and also of black cattle – in case it should please God to
cease the distemper that now rages among them – [to] be from
henceforth hereafter duly opened and held in Battleborough on
Gallow Hill and Brownbank on the first and second day of
June . . .'

Ashbourne (Derbyshire)
Where: Market Place
When: Thursday, Saturday
What: fresh produce, fabrics, footwear, handbags, linen, plants, pet food

Ashbourne Market Place was formerly the scene of every kind of entertainment from bull-baiting and menageries to travelling shows and wandering preachers. Until residents complained about damage to property the Shrovetide football used to be thrown there – the game has now been transferred to Shaw Croft, where on Shrove Tuesday and Ash Wednesday a traditional song is sung, a traditional lunch follows, and then a local celebrity 'turns up' the ball and the game begins. The song goes:

> It is a good old game, deny it if you can
> That tries the pluck of an Englishman.

Two teams are picked from opposite banks of the Henmore river. The goals are three miles apart at Thurston and Clifton, and the object of the game is to move or 'hug' the ball to your own goal and tap it three times on the stone plinth (Clifton) or the mill wheel spindle (Thurston). The person who scores is allowed to keep the ball and the game is stopped at 10 p.m. if no-one has scored. The ball is made of leather, decorated with traditional designs and filled with cork shavings. The winner treasures it as an heirloom.

In the Market Place you can eat at Spencer's Restaurant, and also recommended is Clary's Wine Bar, which is in a very interesting building, a restored workhouse, in nearby Dig St. Ashbourne has long been a market town for the surrounding agricultural district and has a thriving cattle market on Thursdays.

Ashburton (Devon)
Where: the Cattle Market, and the London Inn car-park
When: at the former on Tuesday; at the latter on Thursday
What: both markets sell mainly second-hand goods, bric-à-brac and locally made jewellery

In the Middle Ages Ashburton was a wool market and a stannary town, where tin was brought from the nearby Dartmoor mines to be weighed and valued. The town was governed until 1894 by a portreeve (from the Saxon words '*port*' = market town, and '*gerefa*' = official). The portreeve was witness and recorder of sales of property and cattle. He was also often the only person in a town who could draw up a valid document, and he administered and guaranteed the taking of oaths, fixed dates for court hearings, assessed fines and compensation in cases of theft and false witness, and held deposits of bail. He oversaw church dues and taxes, church fasts and almsgiving. He presided over the Court Leet, but was not a judge – in a Court Leet the jurors are the judges. Another function of the Leet jury was to elect the bailiff, ale-taster and bread-weigher for the town.

Ashburton's first portreeve was elected in 820 and the office exists to this day, though its function is now purely ceremonial. On the Thursday of Carnival week, which starts with a fête on the last Saturday in June and ends with a carnival procession on the first Saturday in July, the ale-taster and bread-weigher go to each inn and bakery in the town to carry out their pleasant duty. The Court Leet and Baron meets on the Annual Court and Law Day at 4 p.m. on the fourth Tuesday in November each year, and the new portreeve, bailiff, ale-taster and bread-weigher are sworn in with the members of the jury.

Ashburton holds a cattle market on the first Thursday of March, April, May, June, August, October and November, and there are a number of attractive inns within easy walk of the market-place.

Ashby-de-la-Zouch (Leicestershire)
Where: Town Hall buildings, Market Street
When: Tuesday, Friday, Saturday
What: general, including antiques and collectors' bargains

A market charter was awarded to the town in 1219 and in the same year Roger la-Zouch gave permission for an annual September

hiring fair, the ancestor of today's funfair. The La-Zouch
Restaurant in Kilwardby Street is recommended for its very
reasonably priced home-cooked food.

Ashford (Kent)
Where: Elwick Road
When: Monday to Saturday
What: cars (Monday); fatstock and calves (Tuesday); dairy cattle,
store cattle, store pigs, hay, straw, standing grass (Wednesday);
horses, tack, machinery, furniture (Thursday); sheep (Friday);
general market (Saturday)

Ashford has the reputation of being in the top three markets in the
British Isles for throughput, with nearly a quarter of a million sheep
annually. Every Saturday there is one of the largest regular general
stall markets in the district, with some 250 stalls attracting 15,000
people.

The new covered sales ring, cafeteria, restaurant and market halls
were completed in May 1978 and opened by Sir Henry Plumb,
President of the National Farmers' Union. The origin of Ashford's
market is a charter of Henry III in 1243. The charter was continued
by Edward III and Charles II, when the market moved from the
High Street to its existing site in Elwick Road. The Company
Registration Number is 118 – Ashford Market is the oldest
registered limited company trading in this country. Shares are
owned by agriculturalists and others interested in the well-being and
prosperity of the market.

Aylesbury (Buckinghamshire)
Where: Friars Square, new town centre
When: Wednesday, Friday, Saturday
What: provisions, fruit, vegetables, plants, clothing, meat, fish,
bric-à-brac

Aylesbury's Old Market Square is a broad expanse of cobblestones surrounded by several ancient coaching inns and dominated by a Victorian Gothic clock tower. However, the market is no longer held here but in the modern centre of Friars Square, whose office blocks overshadow its old home. Lunch near the market can be had in the Old Dark Lantern or the Woolworths Café or Wimpy Bar. Just a short stroll away is the Bell Hotel in Market Square.

Bakewell (Derbyshire)

Where: between the riverside and the town centre
When: Monday
What: food, fruit and vegetables, clothing, shoes, carpets, pets

Bakewell has always been a market town and has the second largest livestock market in the county, after Derby. In 1826 the market was transferred from the streets to its present location, and in 1897 the Urban District Council bought the right to hold the market from the Duke of Rutland. Now 3,000 head of stock can be dealt with in a day. In the eighteenth and nineteenth centuries the market for butter, eggs, pots and pans was held separately, in the market hall or the old town hall, and sometimes in the open air. Today market fairs are held on Easter, Whitsun and August Bank Holidays. Bakewell also has a two-day agricultural show, held in the first week of August.

The correct name for the famous dessert associated with this town is not Bakewell tart but Bakewell pudding. The first Bakewell pudding was an accident – the result of a misunderstanding between the mistress of the Rutland Arms inn, Mrs Greaves, and her cook. Asked to produce a strawberry tart for some important visitors, the cook became flustered and poured egg mixture over the jam, turning the dish into a pudding. The guests were delighted with the originality of the result. The cook confessed her mistake to Mrs Greaves when questioned in private, but was told to carry on producing the puddings. A Bakewell pudding should definitely feature on your menu when you lunch in Bakewell.

Banbury (Oxfordshire)
Where: Market Place
When: Thursday, Saturday
What: vegetables, fruit, clothing, meat, cheese, hardware, dress
materials, jewellery, leather goods, plants, flowers, foam rubber

Banbury is a leading agricultural centre and the Thursday market is
the largest and most important cattle market in Europe, bringing
buyers from all over the world. Banbury is associated with markets
in most people's minds from childhood. Apart from 'Ride a
cock-horse', there are several other nursery rhymes about the town,
among them:

As I was going to Banbury,
Upon a summer's day,
My dame had butter, eggs and fruit,
And I had corn and hay;
Joe drove the ox, and Tom the swine,
Dick took the foal and mare,
I sold them all – then home to dine,
From famous Banbury fair.

and:

Ride a cock-horse
To Banbury Cross,
To see what Tommy can buy;
A penny white loaf,
A penny white cake,
And a two-penny apple pie.

The reason why Banbury appears in so many nursery rhymes, say
Iona and Peter Opie in their *Oxford Dictionary of Nursery Rhymes*,
is possibly that they were printed by a Banbury man, Rusher, who
was eager to promote local business. Banbury Cross was destroyed
by the Puritans in 1602, and the present one was built in 1859.
Banbury cakes, made of flaky pastry and filled with mixed peel,
biscuit crumbs, currants, allspice, eggs and butter, have been
renowned since 1586 and are still to be had in Banbury, though the

original cake shop has now gone. They may be sampled at the
Kopper Kettle, Market Place.

Barnard Castle (Durham)
Where: Market Place
When: Wednesday
What: about 20 stalls selling ladies' lingerie, market-garden
produce, bric-à-brac, infants' clothes, second-hand books, fish,
cheese, carpets, ice-cream, bedding, knitwear, brassware,
protective clothing, meat, garden shears, material, fruit

In the Market Place is the old Town Hall, built in 1747 at the
expense of Thomas Breaks Esq, a Barnard Castle man. The town
council used to meet in the upper part, where the courts were also
held. Farm produce was sold between the pillars on the ground
floor, and it is said that the centre part once served as the local
lock-up. The weather vane has two holes in it, made in 1804 when
two men – Cruddes, a gamekeeper, and Taylor, a Barnard Castle
Volunteer – fired muskets to settle a bet from opposite the Turk's
Head 100 yards away.
   Barnard Castle has a Spring Bank Holiday carnival from Friday
until Monday with sporting events, a fairground, competitions and a
procession featuring several jazz bands.

Barnstaple (Devon)
Where: Market Hall
When: Tuesday and Friday (pannier market); Thursday in the
holiday season (craft market)
What: the pannier market sells local produce, fish (especially locally
caught trout), cheese, books, clothes, bric-à-brac, plants and tools,
as well as crafts; the crafts market is well known for its pottery and
ironwork

There are plenty of pubs nearby; also a restaurant called Settles,
and another in a seventeenth-century building called the Old

Schoolhouse, which is 100 yards away through the churchyard. The pannier market is vibrant and busy, and so called because goods used to be transported to it in panniers. It is well worth a visit. The Market Hall itself dates from 1855. Barnstaple Fair used to be held annually on the Feast of St Mary Magdalene, 22 July. Later it was moved to 8 September, the Feast of the Blessed Virgin. In 1752 when the calendar was revised and eleven days were dropped, the fair was moved to 19 September, on which date it has been held ever since. The early fairs were held in the parish churchyard, with some stalls being set up inside the church porch. It was the custom to go to church first and afterwards visit the fair which attracted all sorts of pedlars, piemen, jugglers, clowns, acrobats – and mountebanks and twisters too. When the fair moved to the castle grounds it was visited by strolling players and prize fighters. There were swings and roundabouts which had to be pushed by hand, and games, including rolling down the castle mound. In the late nineteenth and early twentieth centuries the cattle fair was held on Wednesday and the horse fair on Thursday. Barnstaple was full of farmers and gypsies on these days. As time went by, horse-drawn wagons were replaced with steam engines, beautifully decorated and kept in immaculate condition. Posters in the town warned people against pickpockets and forbade the use of teasers (tickling brushes on wire handles) and confetti.

Today the fair opens on a Wednesday with an ancient custom – at midday a glove, garlanded with flowers, is extended from the Guildhall window to represent a hand of friendship held out in welcome.

Barrow-in-Furness (Cumbria)
Where: Duke Street (indoor market); John Street (open market)
When: Wednesday, Friday, Saturday
What: fruit, vegetables, meat, fish and a large variety of general stalls

The Market Café, facing the open market, offers good food at a low price.

Basildon (Essex)
Where: town centre, near the railway and bus stations
When: Monday, Tuesday, Thursday, Friday, Saturday
What: clothes and general provisions; second-hand goods on
Monday

The Bulls Eye public house is convenient for the market and the
shopping centre. It is a popular place for lunch, offering bar snacks
and a carvery. Basildon Town Show takes place every year on
August Bank Holiday Monday, and is held at Gloucester Park in
the centre of Basildon. It is organized by the Basildon Lions and has
stalls, sideshows, marching bands and majorettes among other
attractions. On the same day a carnival procession with floats winds
its way through Basildon to arrive at the Park.

Basingstoke (Hampshire)
Where: New Market Square and Market Place, in front of the Old
Town Hall
When: Wednesday, Saturday
What: provisions, fresh food, general

Basingstoke has grown to more than six times the size it was in the
1930s because of the overspill from London, and this explains the
necessity for two markets. The New Market Square is adjacent to
the bus station and the pedestrians-only town shopping centre, and
caters for general needs. The old market still exists, with stalls
outside the Old Town Hall, now a museum. The Hop Leaf in
Church Street near the old market is recommended for lunch
because of its friendly atmosphere.

Beccles (Suffolk)
Where: New Market
When: Wednesday, Friday
What: fruit, vegetables, provisions, clothing, shoes, sweets, eggs

Beccles' attractive town sign shows Elizabeth I handing the town's charter to the portreeve, on bended knee before her. The King's Head Hotel can provide a formal lunch, while the White Horse offers bar snacks and cheap roast dinners and fish and chips. Beccles has a summer fair at the Quay; it is also noted for several interesting antique shops around the market, and for the Beccles Auction, which is held on Fridays with pre-sale viewing on Thursdays.

Beverley (North Humberside)
Where: Saturday Market (name of street)
When: Saturday
What: knitwear, antiques, bric-à-brac, cards, jewellery, engraving, eggs, poultry, haberdashery, anoraks, jeans, footwear, fruit, vegetables, basket ware, suiting, clothing, bedding, towels, sweets, biscuits, leather, toys, Nottingham lace, crockery, perfume and cosmetics, radios, watches, dress fabrics, curtaining, foam rubber, glassware, stockings, underwear, hand-made clothes, wool, lino, pet food, office equipment and supplies, tables, pictures, flowers, plants, seeds, household, double-glazing, arts and crafts, carpeting, electrical, motor accessories, wine-making kits, health foods, refreshment van, ice-cream van

A market well worth visiting, not only for the range of goods available, but for the market-place itself, with its fine eighteenth-century buildings and its market cross which dates from 1714 and bears the crests of Queen Anne, Beverley Borough and the Hotham and Warton families, all of whom contributed to the building costs. The King's Head in the market is highly recommended for lunch. Other good pubs nearby are the Green Dragon, also in the market, and the Beaver in North Bar Within.

Bexhill-on-Sea (East Sussex)
Where: Western Road indoor market
When: Tuesday, Friday, Saturday
What: a wide variety includes food, clothing, household and novelties

The nearest pub is the Devonshire in Devonshire Square. There is a carnival on the last weekend in July and a festival of light music on the last weekend in September.

Bicester (Oxfordshire)
Where: Market Square
When: Friday
What: delicatessen, fruit, vegetables, clothes, jewellery

Bicester cattle market is held on Monday and attracts farmers, stock-breeders and dealers from miles around. It also deals in sheep and pigs. There is a sheep fair at Finmere Airfield and an annual funfair on Market Square. Nearby pubs are the Red Lion, the White Hart and the King's Arms.

Bideford (Devon)
Where: Market Place, town centre
When: Tuesday, Saturday
What: a variety of produce and crafts

Charters were granted to Bideford by Elizabeth I and James I. The Bideford regatta and fair, which include rowing events and a carnival, are usually held in the first and second weeks in September. The Edelweiss Hotel is recommended for a good selection of well-presented lunch dishes.

Birkenhead (Merseyside)
Where: Grange Precinct
When: Monday to Saturday
What: general retail

The market was built in 1835, and as the town grew a larger market was opened in 1845; in 1909 part of the open market was covered. In 1974 a new market was opened as part of a shopping complex.

The most popular shopping days are Wednesday, Friday and
Saturday, when the casual miscellaneous and country produce
markets are held. There are several snack bars in the shopping
precinct and around the market, and three pubs, the Garrick Snug,
the Hilton and the Argyll.

Birmingham
Birmingham has four main markets:

Where: Bull Ring
When: Monday to Saturday
What: meat, fruit, vegetables, provisions, carpet, lino, hardware,
clothes, fish, poultry, plants, and many other stalls

Where: Rag, Row and Flea Markets, Edgbaston Street
When: Tuesday, Friday, Saturday, and see below
What: Rag Market – general retail, antiques (see below); The Row
– teenage clothes; Flea Market – all kinds of second-hand goods,
but not clothes

There is a record of a charter granted to Peter de Bermingham by
Henry II in 1166 to hold a market at his castle and to charge tolls.
Birmingham owes much of its prosperity to its early markets, which
expanded over the centuries until they covered more than nine
acres in 1962, when the new Bull Ring opened. This is a colourful
open-air market under the Inner Ring Road with flower-sellers
lining the route to the main city shopping centre. The St Martin's
Rag Market, which has 560 stalls under one roof and attracts traders
from as far away as Derby, Manchester and Nottingham, is noted
for its very cheap new and second-hand goods of all descriptions – a
paradise for bargain hunters. The antiques market is held here on
Mondays and attracts dealers from all over the country and from
abroad. One hundred and fifty stalls sell direct to the public after
the early morning dealer-to-dealer business is concluded. Antique
fairs are held here on four Wednesdays, usually in March, June,
September and December, from 3 to 8 p.m. The Row specializes in

teenage fashion and the flea Market sells old tools and household implements, second-hand furniture, old toys, bric-à-brac, junk, arts and crafts, paintings, prints, pottery, stamps, coins and medals.

The Bull Ring Shopping Centre, opened in 1964, was a multi-million-pound development which provided the city with the most advanced shopping centre in the world and has been a model for others here and abroad. There are plenty of places to eat in the market, and the Matador Public House overlooking the Bull Ring open market can be recommended for its position and reasonable prices.

Bishop Auckland (Co. Durham)
Where: Market Place
When: Thursday, Saturday
What: fruit, clothing, materials, bric-à-brac, soft furnishings – on 140 stalls

Bishop's Castle (Shropshire)
Where: covered market in the Old School in Church Street; livestock market in Station Street near the town centre
When: Friday; some special livestock sales on Thursday and Saturday
What: a very large livestock market, dealing with cattle and hill sheep in season. The covered market has one stall for each of the following: vegetables; eggs, cheese, ham and bacon; antiques, bric-à-brac and some books; fish; plants and garden tools; health foods; home-made cakes; nearly-new clothing; occasional charity stall

This is a very friendly market town in an area where a great deal of food is produced – milk, meat, eggs, cereals and potatoes. Most pubs are open all day on market day, and recommended for lunch are Castle Hotel (AA Relais Routiers); the Three Tuns (for its home-brewed beer); the Number One Coffee Shop and Restaurant in the High Street opposite the market (for vegetarian dishes); the

Boar's Head and King's Head in Church Street (for their proximity
to the livestock market); and the Black Lion in Welsh Street.

On August Bank Holiday Bishop's Castle attracts 25,000 visitors
to a steam-engine rally. On Sunday evening engines and
steam-organs are to be seen in the main street and in pub yards – a
sight enthusiasts will relish.

There has been a market in Bishop's Castle since the Bishop of
Hereford's charter in 1203. A royal charter was granted in 1573.

Bishop's Stortford (Hertfordshire)
Where: Market Square
When: Thursday (when the market is also in North Street in the
town centre), Saturday
What: fresh produce, linen, household goods, toiletries, plants,
tinned goods

The George is recommended for its good food and reasonable
prices.

There are also other local markets: Buntingford (Market Square
at the junction of the A10 and A507) on Monday; Ware (Kibes
Lane car-park off New Road) on Tuesday; and Hertford Market, in
the town centre, on Saturday. In Buntingford, try the Crown or
Jolly Sailors; in Ware, the Saracens Head; and in Hertford, the Old
Barge, Folly Island.

Bletchley (Buckinghamshire)
Where: Queensway
When: Thursday, Friday, Saturday
What: fruit, vegetables, clothing, books, kitchen equipment, etc.

Bletchley is famous for a ceremony known as the Fenny Poppers.
The Poppers are six small cannon, which look like quart-sized
tankards and each take a 4-oz charge of powder. The Poppers are
fired at midday, 2 p.m. and 4 p.m. on St Martin's Day at the Leon

recreation ground. In keeping with tradition, the first and last Poppers are fired by the vicar of St Martin's.

The tradition of the Fenny Poppers goes back to about 1730, when Browne Willis built St Martin's church, Fenny Stratford, in memory of his grandfather, a famous physician by the name of Dr Thomas Willis, who had lived in London in St Martin's Lane and died on St Martin's Day, 1675. When the church was completed, Browne Willis arranged for a sermon to be preached there every St Martin's Day and somehow, though no record exists to show why, the Fenny Poppers came to be fired on the same day. What is certain is that rent from a house Browne Willis gave to the town was used to pay for both the sermon and the gunpowder.

One of the original Poppers burst in 1857 – a fragment was blown on to the roof of the nearby Bull and Butcher and partly destroyed the roof. Because of this, the Poppers were scrapped as unsafe, but one was sent to the Eagle Foundry in Northampton and in 1859 new Poppers were forged from gunmetal and bored by the foundry. These are the Poppers used today. A red-hot rod is used to ignite the powder through the touch holes of the Poppers, which are seven inches long and weigh about 19 lbs. The Poppers were also used at other celebrations – coronations, jubilees and victories – and in 1901 they were used to mourn the death of Queen Victoria. They were fired eighty-one times, to mark her age, and could be heard at Olney, twelve miles away.

The Poppers ceremony creates a great deal of interest and draws about 200 spectators per firing.

Bognor Regis (West Sussex)
Where: Station Yard
When: Saturday
What: cheese, sweets, clothes, household goods, leather

The market at Bognor Regis has been going only since 1981. There is also a carnival on the last Saturday in July and a gala on the last weekend in August. The International Birdman Rally is held in August as well. Market shoppers can pause for refreshment at the Terminus, Station Road.

Boston (Lincolnshire)
Where: Bargate Green; the Market Place
When: Bargate Green, Wednesday; the Market Place, Wednesday,
Saturday
What: both general markets

A document dating from 1207 names the town 'St Botolph's', after
the man who founded a monastery there in the seventh century.
The strong religious connections continued through the Middle
Ages as the market grew in size, and a considerable number of
abbeys and priories traded their wool in the town for provisions.
Boston became a major port: in the thirteenth century, large
quantities of fish were bought at the market for the King's table.
The influence of trade with the Low Countries can be seen in some
of the town's architecture. Religion and the sea, two strands of
Boston's early history, were brought together in the church: from
the tall octagonal tower a beacon shone for the benefit of boats
approaching the harbour.

   Boston did not remain so fortunate, however: by the eighteenth
century the harbour had silted up.

Bradford (West Yorkshire)
Where: John Street Market in John Street; Rawson Market in
Rawson Place; Kirkgate Market in the Arndale Centre, Kirkgate;
fish market in James Street
When: Monday to Saturday, half-day Wednesday
What: John Street – household goods, clothing, confectionery,
greengrocery; Rawson Place – fish, greengrocery, meat; Kirkgate –
household goods, clothing

Bradford no longer has an open-air market, though one existed
until the late 1960s. Its four indoor markets are in modern
buildings, two having been moved from old buildings that were
demolished.

Braintree (Essex)
Where: Market Square, Little Square
When: Wednesday, Saturday
What: vegetables, fruit, fabrics, dresses, fish, food, electrical, bric-à-brac, jewellery, toys

The Braintree carnival is held in June. The Bull, the Nag's Head and Manhattan are all near the market.

Brighton (East Sussex)
Where: Upper Gardener Street
When: Saturday morning
What: fruit, vegetables, flowers, clothing, bric-à-brac and general provisions, but the market specializes in antiques, including jewellery, silver, medals, coins, books, porcelain, ivory, furniture, clocks, glassware and commemorative items

Brighton's oldest quarter is The Lanes, seventeenth-century fishermen's cottages that are now mostly antique shops. The Saturday morning antique market provides a cheaper alternative, promising good bargains. There is also a market every Sunday at Brighton Station from 10 a.m. to 2 p.m., which sells food, clothing and gifts and also has car-boot sales. As a seaside town, Brighton has a huge variety of eating places, too many to single out any.

Bridgnorth (Shropshire)
Where: High Street
When: Saturday
What: meat, groceries, china, leather goods

The Shakespeare Inn in Castle Street is recommended for its good food and good beer. The cattle market is held on Mondays at Smithfield in Whitburn Street. Bridgnorth holds a festival on Spring Bank Holiday Monday with a carnival, market stalls and a procession of floats, and there is a 22-mile sponsored walk to Clee Hill. On the third Sunday in June there is a raft race with 200 rafts travelling from Ironbridge to Bridgnorth.

Bridgwater (Somerset)
Where: Cornhill
When: Wednesday, Friday, Saturday
What: vegetables, fruit, plants, flowers, dairy produce (excellent selection of cheeses), materials, sweets, wholefoods, basket-work (willows), fish, clothes, crockery, wool, books, second-hand stall, haberdashery, toiletries, household goods

Bridgwater has an excellent market and is also famed for its two fairs. St Matthew's Fair is a four-day event taking place in the last week in September, which has one of the largest funfairs in the country and stalls all along West Street selling everything from saucepans to clothes, tinned foods and sweets (no perishables). A sheep and pony sale is held on the first day of this fair. The Bridgwater Carnival, the largest in Somerset, takes place on the Thursday nearest to 5 November. After the evening procession there is 'squibbing' with special fireworks in High Street.

Places for lunch in Bridgwater are the Old Vicarage, a lovely medieval building serving good food; and Sugar and Spice, a café that caters especially for children.

Bridlington (Humberside)
Where: King Street
When: Wednesday, Saturday
What: fresh provisions, household goods. Bridlington is an excellent place for fresh fish, brought straight from the catch and landed at the harbour

Bridport (Dorset)
Where: town centre (East, West and South Streets)
When: Wednesday, Saturday
What: meat, vegetables, bric-à-brac, pictures, jewellery, clothes, household goods, antiques (Saturday is the best day for this), crafts

Market stalls used to cluster round the White Friars' Chapel of St Andrew on the site of the present Town Hall. After the Reformation the chapel fell into disuse, but the building was kept because the tower held the town clock and bells. By the mid-eighteenth century the area had become very congested with traffic trying to negotiate the butchers' shambles, and the site was cleared for the building of a market house, which was opened in 1786. It had 37 butchers' stalls on its ground floor and council offices and courtrooms above. Changing patterns of trade later took the butchers into shops and the open market space was blocked off by bricking in the arches. Today Bridport's market stalls line its wide and spacious central streets.

The Greyhound in East Street is an attractive place for lunch – it dates from about 1300. The George Hotel in South Street has freshly prepared food and good coffee; the Bull in East Street offers a comprehensive bar and restaurant menu; and in West Street Monique's Wine Bar serves English, Continental and vegetarian food. The West End Dairy, also in West Street, has a reasonably priced roast of the day.

Bridport has a carnival procession on the Saturday preceding the August Bank Holiday and a torchlight procession on the Sunday after it, when there is also a fireworks display at West Bay. The Melplash Agricultural Show is held on the last Thursday in August.

Bristol
Where: Corn Street, High Street, St Nicholas Street
When: Monday to Saturday
What: flowers, fruit, vegetables, natural foods, provisions, antiques, bric-à-brac

Bristol's origins go back to Anglo-Saxon times, the settlement growing up round its harbour on the River Avon. The Exchange Hall, built in 1743, stands in the old part of Bristol and is still in use today. On the pavement outside are four bronze pillars called The Nails, on which merchants made their transactions, and which gave rise to the saying 'paying on the nail'. Bristol is home to the World

Bromsgrove

Wine Festival (July), the Hot Air Balloon Festival (August), and the Beer Festival (October), and it holds a Hospital carnival procession in November.

The Rummer and the Crown are good pubs near the market, or there is Carwardine's Coffee House. All are inns of historical interest.

Bromsgrove (Hereford and Worcester)
Where: Market Hall, St John Street
When: Tuesday, Friday, Saturday
What: produce and general, but see below

1987 saw a new market opening in Bromsgrove on the site of the old one in St John Street. It is an unusual market in that it features produce auctions on Tuesday and Friday, where fruit and vegetables can be bought at very reasonable prices. On Wednesday the market is devoted to antiques, and a car auction is held every Monday evening. On the Saturday nearest to 24 June is the Court Leet, an ancient form of administration brought to life in a colourful procession with the bailiff and other notables in their regalia, with ale-tasting and bread-weighing.

There are many pubs in High Street nearby.

Buckingham (Buckinghamshire)
Where: Market Place
When: Tuesday, Saturday
What: a small market with a variety of produce, clothing, household goods and textiles

The manor of Buckingham is recorded in the Domesday Book, but Buckingham did not receive its first royal charter until 1554. This was granted by Queen Mary and confirmed by another charter dated 1684 from Charles II. The Market Square formerly had its own bull ring. In it stands the late seventeenth- or early eighteenth-century Town Hall with its clock tower surmounted by a gilded swan, Buckingham's emblem. The White Hart Hotel, which was an eighteenth-century coaching inn, has a handsome Victorian front and adjoins a terrace of Georgian houses. At the opposite side of Market Square is the thirteenth-century chantry of St John which was rebuilt in 1475 and converted into the Latin School endowed by Edward VI in the sixteenth century. It now belongs to the National Trust. In Market Hill stands a grim building that looks like a castle – this was the old gaol, built in 1748 and now an antique shop.

Buckingham holds a pancake race on Shrove Tuesday, when the townspeople compete with the inhabitants of Glencairn, Ontario, Canada, in synchronized contests for a winner's cup.

Bungay (Suffolk)
Where: The Buttercross, town centre
When: Wednesday, Thursday
What: fruit, vegetables, clothes, trinkets, jewellery

Bungay is a town of many pubs, of which the White Lion in Earsham Street is to be recommended.

Burgess Hill (West Sussex)
Where: Civic Way car-park, near the library (town centre)
When: Wednesday, Saturday
What: fruit, vegetables, clothes, antiques

Burgess Hill in one of the major shopping centres of West Sussex.

Burnley (Lancashire)
Where: Market Hall and Open Market
When: Monday, Wednesday, Thursday, Friday, Saturday (indoors); Monday, Thursday, Saturday (outdoors)
What: both markets are large, the indoor market having 119 stalls, and the outdoor market, which is partly glazed, having 143, so a wide variety of goods is on sale

An antiques and bric-à-brac market is held in the Open Market on Wednesdays. The annual Pot Fair comes to Burnley in the summer holidays and attracts traders in china and glass from all over the country. The markets and fairs of Burnley were first established during the reign of Edward I, who granted them to Henry de Lacy, Lord of the Manor, in 1294. The market rights were taken over by the Corporation in 1866. The first market hall was opened in 1870, but was demolished to make way for the new Market Hall in 1969.

Bury (Greater Manchester)
Where: Market Hall
When: Wednesday, Friday, Saturday
What: a large general market with a huge choice of fresh quality produce and bargains, but the speciality is the black pudding stall

The original charter to hold a weekly market on Fridays and two three-day fairs was granted in 1440 by Henry VI to Sir John Pilkington, Lord of the Manor of Bury. The oldest building in Bury is probably the Two Tubs in the Market Place, which dates from the early eighteenth century. In 1949 it was discovered that the Two Tubs had been built round two giant oak trees, probably from the time of Charles II. Bury market has been in the new Market Hall since 1971, but the smell of traditional hot black puddings, the local delicacy for well over a century, still wafts appetizingly through the stalls and draws visitors from all over the world.

Bury St Edmunds (Suffolk)
Where: Buttermarket and Cornhill, town centre
When: Wednesday, Saturday
What: fresh fruit and vegetables, fish, bric-à-brac, clothes, coins, lampshades, plants, flowers, fabrics, key-cutting, hot dogs, toys

This ancient market and cathedral town is called after the martyred Saxon king, St Edmund, whose remains were enshrined in the monastery here thirty-three years after his death in 870. The Domesday Book of 1086 reveals that the wide open space outside the convent's main gate was used as a fairground and a market for butter, horses, beasts and corn. By the thirteenth century the town had developed its trade to become one of the leading cloth and agricultural centres in the country. Today the market still thrives on its ancient site, though Bury's main industries are brewing and sugar-beet.

The Cupola House in the Traverse is recommended for a pub lunch. It has been described as the best seventeenth-century house in the town with a handsome façade, magnificent open staircase and a fine cupola on the roof, which gives it its name.

Buxton (Derbyshire)
Where: Market Place, Higher Buxton
When: Saturday all year, Tuesday from April to December
What: fruit, vegetables, linen, fabrics, shoes, fish, meat

Buxton has been a spa town since Roman times, with unusually pleasant-tasting water. St Anne's Well in the centre of town is the focal point of the July carnival and Well Dressing. For those not taking the waters there are several pubs in the market place.

Caernarfon (Gwynedd)
Where: Market Hall, Palace Street; open market, Market Square
When: Market Hall, daily; open market, Saturday
What: fruit, vegetables, provisions, clothes, household goods

Caernarfon has an annual Christmas Fair. Pubs recommended near the market are the Albert Inn, the Black Boy Inn and the Crown.

Caerphilly (Mid Glamorgan)
Where: Pentrebane Street
When: Monday to Saturday
What: fruit, vegetables, meat, sweets, wool, clothing, cheese

Caerphilly to most people means a crumbly white cheese with a distinctive tang. Cheeses from local farms were marketed in the town from about 1316 until 1910 – but now Caerphilly cheese is made in Somerset. So as not to disappoint visitors, special one-pound cheeses are transported from Somerset to Caerphilly and sold in the market with a sticker saying that the cheese was at least *bought* in Caerphilly. An information sheet containing the history of the cheese and a recipe for making it is available from the Tourist Information Centre in Park Lane. Each June there is a Medieval Fayre organized by the Caerphilly Round Table and held in the castle grounds. Visitors to the market are directed to the King's Head, the Railway and the Courthouse, all nearby pubs.

Cambridge
Where: Market Square
When: Monday to Saturday
What: fruit, particularly excellent vegetables, fabrics, clothes, second-hand books, unusual selection of records, dried flowers in profusion, fish, fresh flowers, plants, bulbs

Cambridge began with the Romans, who built a camp beside the River Cam. By the fifth century it had become a Saxon market town, and not until the thirteenth century did it become a centre of learning. The Midsummer Fair has been held on the Midsummer Common since the Middle Ages, and begins with the mayor distributing pennies to children. The Eagle pub near the market is recommended for its friendly atmosphere.

  Today's market is small and intimate, held under bright awnings on the cobbled square. Of particular interest are the book and record stalls. There are at least three stalls selling dried flowers – a huge array of very unusual and attractive varieties, reasonably priced.

Cannock (Staffordshire)
Where: town centre
When: Tuesday, Friday, Saturday
What: meat, fish, vegetables, fruit, clothing, shoes, plants, bric-à-brac

The right to hold a Tuesday market and an annual fair on the Feast of St Michael (15–17 October) was granted to Cannock by Henry III and confirmed in 1293.

Canterbury (Kent)
Where: Kingsmead Road
When: Monday to Saturday
What: food, haberdashery, toys, junk, fabrics

Canterbury is a small city, not more than a mile across, bordered by a wall. It affords little space for a large market, and no record of a market charter has ever been found, but there is plenty of evidence that there were a number of small markets here. The Kingsmead market opened in 1983. A cattle market is held on Mondays in Market Way, St Stephens. The forerunner of this market was held in St George's parish outside the city walls from 1580 to 1955. In the early years of this century sheep and cattle were still driven to market along the road outside the wall.

The old corn market used to be in St Andrew's parish near the church. In 1824 it was moved to Longmarket, beside the butchers' shambles. Vegetables were sold downstairs. In 1938 this building was turned into an assembly hall, and in 1942 it was bombed – plans have recently been put forward for its restoration.

Canterbury was granted a charter to act as the centre of the hop trade by George III in 1766. Hops were sold in the corn market. The town had a flourishing fish market by 1200, and it even has a fishermen's church: St Mary Burgate. There was a separate market for Whitstable fish. In 1620 these two markets were amalgamated – the pump in Pykenot Alley was installed by the corporation behind this market in 1631 for the washing of fish. In 1892 the building, which still stands, was converted into two shops; it was last used as a fish shop in 1983.

At the market cross bulls were baited and poultry, game and vegetables sold on Wednesday and Saturday. A rush market was held at the back gate of the Archbishop's palace at Redewell; there was a wheat market in St Paul's parish outside Burgate; a shambles in Butchery Lane (where you can still see the plaster head of a bull above Timpsons); a cloth market in St George's Street; a bread market beside St Mary Bredmans (bakers') church in High Street; a salt market at Oaten Hill; a wine market at Wincheap outside the gate; and a herb market on the site of the Salutation Tavern.

The Canterbury Festival is held in September and October. Pubs near the Kingsmead Road market are Ye Old Beverley and the Jolly Sailor.

Carlisle (Cumbria)
Where: Market Street
When: Monday to Saturday, half-day Thursday
What: fruit, vegetables, provisions, toys, meat, fish, computers. Specialities: market-garden produce, Cumberland sausage

The Carlisle market charter dates from 1158, and tolls levied from stallholders and animal traders were in existence long before that. Gates and shire tolls, which brought revenue from all who entered the city and county, were abandoned only in 1949, when modern transport finally defeated their collection. Carlisle's importance as a market town owes much to the fact that it serves such a large area. Sellers used to pitch their stalls in the open street or in front of the Moot Hall. In 1799 the butchers were the first to get covered accommodation in the shambles, which remains to this day. Despite persistent demand, the Covered Market was not erected until ninety years later, when there was great rejoicing, a torchlight procession and a fireworks display. Today the Market is also used for dog shows, exhibitions, dances, symphony concerts, badminton, netball, boxing and wrestling. There is a Market Cafeteria and in nearby Fisher Street is the King's Head.

The Great Fair is held each year on 26 August and proclaimed by the clerk and chief executive reading the original charter from the Town Hall steps at 8 a.m. This ceremony, which has taken place annually for more than 150 years, is attended by the mayor, town clerk, chief of police, markets superintendent and sword and mace bearers. The civic dignitaries wear traditional robes, and process to the market cross. Before 1975 the official party then resumed ordinary dress and repaired to the Market Coffee Tavern for a large breakfast of bacon and eggs. Since that date, however, an official breakfast has been attended by 150 people in the Tithe Barn, an ancient building which has been restored by the city and is used for all kinds of events.

The Covered Market itself is a Victorian construction with a three-arch span and a glazed roof based on early Renaissance style. The roof is more than sixty feet high and supported by a cast-iron framework. One of the spans originally covered a casual market for country people, and this is where the dog shows, etc, are held today. The Market has been very sensitively restored, and as many of the original features have been kept as was possible – for example, the original marble fish slabs have been built into modern units.

There is always a list of eighty to a hundred people waiting to occupy the permanent stalls in the fish market, butchers' shambles and general market, and a close watch is kept to maintain a competitive balance, taking into account the needs of the people of Carlisle and the surrounding area.

Carmarthen (Dyfed)
Where: end of Red Street Precinct
When: Monday to Saturday; open-air market Wednesday, Saturday
What: general groceries, household goods, books, antiques, home-grown and farm produce, fish

Carmarthen was granted a royal charter by King John in 1201, but the town goes back beyond Roman times to the days when it was a Celtic hill fort. It is claimed to be the home of King Arthur's wizard Merlin and one of the earliest eisteddfods was held here in 1451. On the River Towy salmon is caught in nets strung between coracles, ancient boats whose use is as old as Carmarthen itself. Local salmon is a delicacy well worth looking for in the market.

The present market was opened in 1846, before which time goods were sold in various parts of town: meat, poultry and cheese in John

Street, corn beneath the Guildhall, boots, hardware and hats in Guildhall Square, fish and butter in Nott Square, and pigs in Lammas Street. At the beginning of this century the market featured cocklewomen, ropemakers, woodworkers, churn-makers, clogmakers and tin-men, all of whom have sadly since disappeared, like the town crier. Farmers drove to town, stabled their horses in the pub yards and lined their carts up along the street.

Cheltenham (Gloucestershire)
The three general markets in Cheltenham provide for most needs:
Where: Market Street (off Gloucester Road)
When: Thursday morning
What: about sixty stalls selling general goods

Where: Winchcombe Street (indoor market complex)
When: Tuesday to Saturday
What: more than thirty traders in small, inter-connected shops

Where: Winchcombe Street
When: Friday, Saturday
What: market stalls on the pavement in front of the indoor complex

Chesterfield (Derbyshire)
Where: Market Place and Market Hall
When: Monday, Thursday, Friday, Saturday
What: fish, meat, fruit, vegetables, dress fabrics, curtains, provisions, clothes, confectionery. Thursday: antiques, collectors' items, bric-à-brac

Chesterfield's Market Place has been renovated and there is also a covered market in the Market Hall. In July is the annual medieval market and funfair, recalling the town's medieval past which remains in some of the street names, such as Knifesmith Gate and Glumangate (a gluman or gleeman was a minstrel). There is also a charity market where funds are raised by various means, including entertainment and increased rents to stallholders. Nearby, Mr C's Restaurant is a family eating-place recommended by Egon Ronay.

Chester-le-Street (Co. Durham)
Where: town centre
When: Tuesday, Friday (212 stalls), Saturday
What: a general market with all kinds of goods on Tuesday and Friday, and a flea market on Saturday

Chichester (West Sussex)
Where: Cattle Market, off Market Avenue
When: Wednesday and Saturday mornings
What: livestock and general on Wednesday; general on Saturday

Chichester has been a market town at least since Roman times. The City Cross in the centre was the original market cross, built in 1501 of Caen stone, the gift of Bishop Storey. It was used by country people who brought their goods to market until 1807, when the Butter Market or Market House came into service. This colonnaded building in North Street, designed by John Nash, is still in use by small traders today. Its predecessor in North Street was the medieval market hall, a timber-framed building that appears to have stood in the middle of the street. The alleyway leading from Macari's in North Street to St Martin's Street was known as the Shambles, with butchers' stalls set up in the narrow space. St Martin's Street itself was known as Hog Lane, since that was where the hog market was held; the cattle market was held in what is now the car-park behind Marks and Spencer, near St Andrew Oxmarket. Leather-selling was centred on the Pallant. When the beast market outgrew the back streets it was moved to East Street, and has been held at its present position since 1872. In about 1830 the Corn Exchange was built in East Street: it is now used for shops and offices. Apart from the theatre festival, which runs from April to October, there is a gala on the first Saturday in July and the Sloe Fair at the end of October.

Chippenham (Wiltshire)
Where: Bath Road
When: Friday
What: food, haberdashery, clothes, bric-à-brac, antiques, gifts, stationery

Chippenham Women's Institute contributes home-made preserves, cakes and home-grown vegetables to the food section of this market. Chippenham has been an important market town since the fourteenth century and still holds one of the biggest cattle markets in the country – at Cocklebury Rd on Fridays. The Yelde Hall in the market place, with its wooden turret, dates from the fifteenth century and is now the town's museum.

Chipping Norton (Oxfordshire)
Where: Market Place, town centre
When: Wednesday
What: a small market with only 15 traders, but they offer a good variety of high-standard wares

The name 'Chipping Norton' derives from the Anglo Saxon *ceapen* – to cheapen or to buy, and this ancient settlement was thus known as 'the Market of the North Town'. The name 'Cheping Norton' is first recorded in a royal writ of 1244. In the Middle Ages the town's prosperity was founded on the wool trade, and tweed from the wool of Cotswold sheep was still made until 1980. There is a good choice of eating places near the market.

Chorley (Lancashire)
Where: Flatiron Market, Clissord Street; general market, Market Place
When: Flatiron, Tuesday; general market, Tuesday, Friday, Saturday
What: Flatiron has 115 stalls selling clothing, linen, towels, books, fancy goods, etc; general market is mostly fresh food

Cirencester (Gloucestershire)
Where: Market Place
When: Monday, Friday
What: fruit, cheese, clothes, electrical goods, plants, health foods, meat, fish, leather goods, fancy goods

The Black Horse is recommended as a pub of character for lunch. The Cirencester carnival is held at the first weekend in July, and the Mop Fair is held in October.

Clitheroe (Lancashire)
Where: Market Place
When: Tuesday, Saturday
What: fish, meat, vegetables, clothes, carpets, jewellery, make-up, cakes, toys, sweets

Victoria Hotel and White Lion Hotel offer refreshment in the Market Place, and the Market Café is in Market Street. Clitheroe holds a heritage fair in June, a traditional craft market in August, and a torchlight procession and castle fête in September.

Cockermouth (Cumbria)
Where: Market Place
When: Monday
What: fruit and vegetables, general household goods

The Black Bull offers good-value pub lunches. Cockermouth, Wordsworth's birthplace, has fairs at Whitsun and Martinmas, and an agricultural show in August.

Congleton (Cheshire)
Where: Market Hall off Victoria Street
When: Tuesday, Saturday
What: a large market of 100 stalls, some indoors, most out

A Saturday market has been held at Congleton since the rights were first granted to Henry de Lacey in 1282. By 1859 the rights had passed to Sir C. W. Shakerley, who transferred them to the local authority. Stalls were set up in the main streets in the early years but in 1866 the traders moved to covered accommodation in the Town Hall. In 1959 the market moved to new premises, but soon outgrew them and the present market off Victoria Street was opened in 1981, combining traditional design with a high standard of efficiency and cleanliness.

There is a cattle market on Tuesday in Macclesfield Road. Every 'even' year the Congleton Carnival and Tattoo takes place on the Spring Bank Holiday weekend, and each 'odd' year it is the turn of the Heritage Fayre.

Conwy (Gwynedd)
Where: Market Place
When: Tuesday, Saturday
What: fruit, vegetables, provisions, fabrics, clothes, meat, plants

Besides the general goods on offer in the market, fresh fish and mussels can be bought at stalls on the Quay.

Corby (Northamptonshire)
Where: Market Square
When: Thursday (30 stalls), Friday (90 stalls), Saturday (90 stalls)
What: a comprehensive range of goods from food to clothes and household items

Corby holds an unexpected kind of carnival for a Northamptonshire town – an annual Highland Gathering and Fun Day in July. This features market and charity stalls as well as competitions for dancing, piping and drumming, and haggis hurling and eating.

The Market Plaice Fish Restaurant and the Corby Candle offer lunch to market visitors.

Coventry (West Midlands)
Where: Queen Victoria Road
When: Monday to Saturday, half-day Thursday
What: fruit, vegetables, dress and curtain fabrics, footwear, flowers, plants, meat, excellent fish stalls, pet foods, crockery, jewellery, clothes, towels, bedding

Coventry's market charter dates from 1348. The market was held at Cross Cheaping (*cheaping* was a market), and there were a number of benches in the open around the market cross. In 1719 a market house was erected, superseded by a market hall in 1867, which was in use until the Blitz in 1940, when it and much of the rest of Coventry were destroyed. The scattered market traders used various temporary sites after the War until 1958 when they were rehoused in the present circular building. The opening of the new market by Princess Alexandra marked a significant stage in the reconstruction of the city centre. It also attempted to relieve central traffic congestion by incorporating a car-park on its roof. The market has a children's play area and a roundabout. There are refreshments in the market at the Market Tavern, and the Swiss Alps Restaurant is nearby.

   Coventry's annual Great Fair starts on the Friday before the Spring Bank Holiday and runs until the following Saturday, when there are fireworks. The carnival procession features a 'nude' Lady Godiva astride a white horse.

Crawley (West Sussex)
Where: Orchard Street
When: Tuesday, Thursday, Friday, Saturday
What: clothing, fish, groceries, vegetables

The George Hotel, High Street, was built in 1615. It has a coffee shop and serves good bar lunches.

Crewe (Cheshire)
Where: Earle Street
When: every day (half-day Wednesday) in the Market Hall; Friday,
Saturday, Monday morning in the open air
What: everything from food to hardware

The town of Crewe was created by the railways. The market has
recently been extensively renovated. Dilapidated buildings have
been demolished to make more room for open-air stalls, but the
Market Hall, a Grade II listed building housing 46 lock-up stalls,
has been preserved.

Crewe has a carnival on the third Saturday in August with stands
and stalls, dancing, sky-diving, helicopter displays, fire-eaters,
grass-track racing, pet shows, escapologists, daredevil artists and a
funfair. Places to eat in Crewe are the Royal Hotel and the Crewe
Arms, both in Nantwich Road.

Darlington (Co. Durham)
Where: Market Place in the town centre; cattle market in Clifton
Road
When: covered market, Monday to Saturday; open market,
Monday, Saturday; cattle market, Monday, Thursday
What: clothing, stationery, second-hand books, footwear, fish,
animal foodstuffs, plants, seeds, agricultural equipment, fruit,
vegetables, meat (pork pies a speciality)

Darlington is first mentioned in the first decade of the eleventh
century as a 'market towne in the bishoprike of Durham'. As early
as 1315 its importance as a market for corn and cattle drew
travelling merchants from distant parts. In 1532 it was recorded that
market day was Monday – it still is today. From the very early days
until 1854 one or two men stood at each entrance to the town to
collect the tolls and had power of seizure in case of non-payment.
The open market was held in the vicinity of St Cuthbert's church
and a market cross was built there in 1577, near which stood a
wooden toll booth. Funeral processions used to rest at the cross on

their way to the churchyard. The present cross, erected in 1727, stands on the same site and is unusual in that it is now inside a covered market. Darlington's fairs are even older than the market, and used to be the occasion of hiring farm labour. Now they are given over to shows and amusements, and they take place at Easter and in autumn.

The Bull's Head Inn, Market Place, has been used for centuries by visitors to the market, and serves excellent lunches.

Dartmouth (Devon)
Where: Market Square off Victoria Road
When: Tuesday, Friday
What: all types of food, shoes, pictures, bric-à-brac

The Market House Inn provides good food at a reasonable price and the annual fatstock show is held in December.

Daventry (Northamptonshire)
Where: Market Square
When: Tuesday, Friday
What: fruit and vegetables, general provisions, household goods, materials, clothes

A weekly market was first held in Daventry in 1255, with a two-day fair on St Augustine's Day. Throughout the Middle Ages, Daventry market handled agricultural produce from the surrounding area. Queen Elizabeth I's charter of 1576 allowed for a further two-day fair on the Feast of St Matthew the Apostle. Today's descendants of these fairs are the spring and autumn Mop Fairs which each last for a full week. The Market Square retains much of the character of Old Daventry with the fine eighteenth-century Church of the Holy Cross, and the Moot Hall dating from the same period. Two old coaching inns, the Wheat Sheaf with its long white frontage and the Saracen's Head built around an attractive courtyard, are recommended for lunch, along with the Windsor Lodge in New Street.

Denbigh (Clwyd)
Where: High Street
When: Wednesday
What: various, but no open food allowed. Livestock markets are
held on Wednesday

You can eat at the fifteenth-century Golden Lion Inn nearby.

Derby
Derby today has six markets, three general and three specialist:

Eagle Centre Market (city centre): opens on Tuesday, Thursday,
Friday and Saturday. There are 321 stalls selling general provisions,
clothing, toys, fancy goods and flowers. Specialities are shoe repairs
and hairdressing. Mr J. Diner, who sells rainwear on stalls 47E and
47F has been trading in the market for fifty-one years.
Market Hall (city centre): opens Monday to Saturday, half-day on
Wednesday. It sells fruit, vegetables, provisions, fancy goods and
clothing and specializes in meat, fish, poultry and game.
Allenton Market (four miles from the city centre at Allenton): opens
on Friday and Saturday for general goods, including fruit,
vegetables, other provisions and clothing. On Tuesday evening
there is a flea market here.
Cattle Market (Chequers Road, two miles from the city centre): on
Tuesday there are fatstock auctions and on Friday store stock
auctions. There are also sales by private treaty and special pedigree
sales.
Public Abattoir and Wholesale Meat Market (Chequers Road, two
miles from the city centre): Monday to Friday it offers facilities for
private butchers and wholesalers.
Wholesale Fruit and Vegetable Market (Chequers Road, two miles
from the centre): opens Monday to Saturday for the sale of fruit,
vegetables, flowers and horticultural produce.

Derby gave a home to Britain's first silk mill, which was opened in
1702. It is also famous for Crown Derby porcelain, jewellery,

marble work, soap and brewing. The markets of Derby play a leading role in the character and trade of the town. A market charter was granted to Derby in 1155 and from that day to this the main market day has been a Friday. In 1665 Derby was visited by the plague for the second time: the town was almost deserted and farmers refused to bring their produce to the Market Place. Trade ground to a standstill. To prevent a famine, the dwindled population set up a temporary market at Nun's Green, which at that time was outside the town: market traders gathered here with their provisions and stood chewing tobacco to ward off the germs. They took up their positions at a distance from the goods they had brought to sell so that they did not have to come into contact with their customers. The customers were not allowed to touch anything before buying it and had to deposit the right money in a vessel filled with vinegar. The seller could not check the money, nor the buyer examine his purchase. Both sides had of necessity to trust each other and a mutual confidence was built up that did not exist before and has not, unfortunately, entirely survived.

Devizes (Wiltshire)
Where: Market Place
When: Thursday
What: clothes, antiques, shoes, jewellery, meat, wet fish, dairy produce, gifts

This is the largest market square in the west of England. Devizes was granted its first charter in 1141 by Empress Matilda, mother of Henry II, but much of its prosperity was built on the cloth and wool trade of the eighteenth century. The market cross was erected in 1814 by Henry Addington, later Lord Sidmouth, Prime Minister, and one panel tells the story of Ruth Pierce, a market woman who dropped dead after telling a lie. There is also a fountain built in 1879 in memory of T. H. Sotherton Escourt. The Bear is an old coaching inn dating from 1599, whose most famous landlord was the father of the portrait-painter Sir Thomas Lawrence. The Corn Exchange (1857) is one of the largest public halls in Wiltshire and features a statue of Ceres. The Shambles was built in 1835 as a covered market. On Tuesday there is an antiques market here and on Thursday and Saturday a general market. Devizes Carnival is in August, and there are also festivals of art and music and a car rally – contact Kennet District Council, Bath Road for more details.

The Market Place offers an enormous selection of establishments serving lunch. These are Annie's Café, the Cheesecake tea rooms, the Bear Hotel, the Seafood Restaurant and the Black Swan Hotel. In Monday Market Street is the Fish Takeaway.

Doncaster (South Yorkshire)
Where: Market Place
When: Tuesday, Friday, Saturday; antiques on Wednesday
What: general retail goods, including clothes, fish, vegetables, food, hardware, textiles, ironmongery, toys, confectionery; antiques and crafts on Wednesday

In 1199 King John granted to Robert de Turnham the right to hold a fair in Doncaster on the Feast of St James, 25 July; and in 1467 King Edward IV gave the mayor and community the right to hold a fair on the Feast of the Virgin Mary, 25 March. A market charter was granted in 1664 by Charles II, giving permission for a Saturday market to be held for the buying and selling of oxen, cows, hogs, horses and sheep. The mayor was appointed clerk of the market and a Pie Powder Court (see page 10) was set up to deal with customers' grievances. Cattle were sold in the Market Place, sheep in the Parsonage Yard; skins and hides were first disposed of in the Shambles, then moved to the Corn Market, and then to the lamp post in the centre of the Market Place. Drapers' booths were a feature of Doncaster market from as early as 1310. By 1800 they had established themselves in the Corn Market and were selling 'two shades of drab'. Hay and straw were sold in New Street, but moved from there to the Parsonage Yard, giving up their old place to potato sellers. Earthenware pots were sold from the Magdalens, along with hardware, ready-made clothes, linens, baskets, cooperage and shoes. Butchers set up their shambles around 1608 at

the Butcher Cross in Hallgate, which became High Street. On Whit
Monday of 1847 the foundation stone of a new Market Hall was laid
by the mayor, underneath which were placed coins of Queen
Victoria's reign and several documents, the ceremony being
followed by a public breakfast for 300 people. The Hall was
eventually opened in 1849 for the sale of meat, poultry, butter and
eggs. Doncaster's first market cross was erected in 1634 in the
Market Place on the site of a maypole: market crosses were erected
more as mercantile landmarks than religious symbols, and sellers of
butter and eggs gathered around them.

Places to eat in Doncaster Market Place are Tiffin's (above H. I.
Weldrick the chemist), and the Red Lion.

Dorchester (Dorset)
Where: Cattle Market
When: Wednesday morning
What: a large general market, with a range of bric-à-brac and
second-hand goods

Since Roman times there has been a settlement at Dorchester: a
mint was founded there by the Anglo-Saxons, and a castle was built
at Dorchester by the Normans. Despite the town's eventful early
history, there is less architectural evidence of it than might be
expected, simply because a fire in 1613 destroyed most of the old
buildings.

The market has reached a peak of 400 stalls in the past, though
such a number is not usual. Cattle are sold on Thursdays.

Dorking (Surrey)
Where: Market Place, off High Street
When: Friday
What: goods on sale range from foodstuffs to clothing

Records show that the right to hold a market in Dorking was
granted to the Lord of the Manor as long ago as 1278. The town also

has the right to hold a charter fair on Cotmandene on the eve of Ascension Day and on Ascension Day itself each year. There are many good eating-houses in the High Street, all within easy walking distance of the market. The High Street is the main shopping street and a conservation area. It is a good place for antiques-hunting.

Dudley (West Midlands)
Where: Market Place, town centre
When: Monday to Saturday, half-day Wednesday
What: fruit and vegetables, crockery, materials, greetings cards, pet foods, clothes, household goods

The earliest mention of a market in Dudley is in 1261 when Lord Dudley accused his rival, Giles de Erdington, of setting up a market in Wolverhampton and taking away his trade. In the time of Charles II the right to hold spring and autumn livestock fairs was granted to the town. Today's descendant of these is the Dudley Show held on the outskirts of the town on the first weekend in August, which features a dog show, crafts tents, a horticultural show, a goat show, a fair and horse-riding as well as market stalls. Occasionally the town holds a Black Country Market, an evening event in the open market with stalls taken over by local craftspeople and local societies.

   Recommended eating places are the King Arthur Carvery, Priory Road; the Station Hotel, Castle Hill and the Ward Arms Hotel, Birmingham Road.

Dunstable (Bedfordshire)
Where: Market Place
When: Wednesday, Saturday
What: fruit, vegetables, china, flowers, clothes, jewellery, household wares, gardening equipment, meat, an excellent cheese stall

Present-day Dunstable dates from the twelfth century, when Henry I built the Augustinian priory around which the market town grew. There are several pubs near the market and the Sugar Loaf, which is about five minutes' walk away, is highly recommended. Dunstable carnival is held every Spring Bank Holiday. A day out in Dunstable could also include a visit to Whipsnade Zoo and Whipsnade Tree Cathedral – trees planted in the shape of a cathedral after the First World War.

Eastleigh (Hampshire)
Where: Civic Offices, Leigh Road; and car-park next to Safeways supermarket
When: the former on Sunday; the latter on Thursday
What: vegetables, fruit, provision, plants, clothes, books, materials, shoes, handbags, underwear, jewellery, toys, pet foods, health foods

The Golden Eagle Pub and the Piccolo Mondo Restaurant are recommended for lunch. Carnival week is in August, ending with a procession on the Saturday.

Ellesmere Port (Cheshire)
Where: Wellington Road, Cambridge Road
When: Tuesday, Friday, Saturday
What: 132 stalls and 37 shop units selling fruit, vegetables, fish, meat, flowers, cooked meats, fashions, sweets, pet foods, ex-catalogue and fancy goods

There are two cafés in the market, and the Grace Arms Public House on Stanley Lane is highly recommended for its pleasant friendly atmosphere and varied menu. Fairs are held in the parking area by the market in February, April and September. The size of the market and the fact that there is ample free parking attracts visitors from as far away as Wales.

Ely (Cambridgeshire)
Where: Market Square
When: Thursday
What: fresh produce, clothes, fabric, garden equipment, plants

At the end of the months of May and October there is a funfair in
the Market Place, and on August Bank Holiday Monday is the
Elizabethan Sports and Social Day. The Coffee Mill in Market
Street, and Wraggs and the White Hart Hotel in the Market Square
all serve lunch.

Evesham (Hereford and Worcester)
There are three markets in Evesham:

Where: Market Place
When: Saturday
What: locally grown produce – fruit, vegetables and flowers; general
goods

Where: Market Hall
When: Tuesday, Thursday, Friday, Saturday
What: as Saturday market above

Where: High Street
When: Monday to Friday
What: as Saturday market above

Market gardening was started in the Vale of Evesham by an Italian,
Francis Bernardi, who retired there from Genoa and spent £30,000
planting his land with fruit and vegetables, which he offered for sale
in the markets. Within half a century the town's best land had been
given over to market gardening, the locals being convinced that
their soil was particularly suited to it. William Pitt, writing in 1813
records:

> The inhabitants of Evesham are occupied in the raising of the
> usual garden plants as well as onions, cucumbers and asparagus

for the supply of neighbouring markets. It is a common sight for 60–80 horses to be laden in a day with garden stuff for Birmingham market but the roads being now improved it is sent in wheel carriages with much fewer number of horses.

With the coming of the railways in the 1850s the gardeners had a much wider market and the industry grew apace. Another factor that promoted horticulture in the district was the Evesham custom of land tenure, whereby the outgoing tenant agreed with the incoming tenant the value of crops, manuring and cultivations and received payment accordingly. This made gardeners unafraid to invest in their land as they knew they would be repaid for their efforts. Market gardening remains the prime industry of the Vale of Evesham, but the small family units are fast disappearing in favour of large holdings which can be worked more economically.

The Royal Oak, Vine Street, does bed and breakfast as well as lunches and enjoys a very good reputation.

Exeter (Devon)
Where: St George's Market, Market Street
When: Monday to Saturday
What: fish, meat, confectionery, fruit, vegetables, general foods, butter, eggs, poultry, antiques, toys, clothing, materials, tools, records

Exeter has been an important market town from at least Saxon times, its geographical position making it the agricultural centre for its own and neighbouring counties. Its market charter was granted by Edward I. In South Street was the serge market, with the wool market near the Bear Inn; fish, potatoes and oats were sold in Gandy Street and Little Queen Street; and the pork butchers were in the High Street. In 1820 it was recorded that tar barrels had to be burned there to purify the air. In 1838 the traders were grouped together in a specially constructed market, which was destroyed during the last War and then rebuilt on the same site, with an underground car-park. Today the livestock market is held on

Mondays and Fridays at Marsh Barton, having been moved out of
the city centre in 1939 to improve hygiene and lessen traffic
congestion.

Lammas Fair, held in August, dates back before the Norman
Conquest. It begins today, as it always has done, with a procession
around the city, after which the charter for holding the fair is read
and an enormous white glove is mounted on the highest part of the
Guildhall, in welcome.

Fareham (Hampshire)
Where: Market car-park adjacent to West Street and Quay Street
When: Monday morning
What: vegetables, fruit, cakes, clothes, household goods, toys and
bric-à-brac

In West Street is a choice of fast-food restaurants and a pub called
the Bugle. Fareham Show is held in June, and three miles away at
Titchfield a Bonfire Carnival is held on the last Monday in October.

Farnborough (Hampshire)
Where: Westmead car-park, just off Queensmead shopping centre
When: Tuesday
What: meat, fish, fruit, vegetables, clothing, shoes, dressmaking
materials, workshop tools, crockery, cakes, household utensils,
plants, used paperbacks, toys, and two charity stalls selling
second-hand goods and plants

In Kingsmead shopping centre there are cafés, a wine bar and a
fish-and-chip shop. The Round Table organizes a Donkey Derby
each summer, and Farnborough also hosts the annual Southern
Business Technology and Trade Fair.

Felixstowe (Suffolk)
Where: Town Station Yard; Cavendish Hotel car-park
When: Station Yard market on Thursday; Cavendish Hotel market
on Sunday

What: clothes, fresh fruit, dairy produce, fish, meat, vegetables, shoes, bags

Felixstowe was developed as a seaside resort by the Victorians. There are plenty of cafés and restaurants on the sea-front, and the Cavendish Hotel provides refreshment for Sunday shoppers.

Fishguard (Dyfed)
Where: Town Hall
When: Thursday
What: general market with special attractions in the form of garden produce, local dairy produce and local crafts

The Royal Oak opposite the market comes highly recommended for its good food, good beer and excellent company, and service. Apart from its excellence as a local pub it is also the spot where the French surrendered after the 'Last Invasion of Britain' in February 1797.

Inside the Market Hall is a board with an inscription dated 1836, which details the tolls payable under an Act of Parliament passed in the fourth year of the reign of William IV on 17 June 1834. It includes the following items:

For every stall used by a butcher selling flesh
    meat being his own property 1s 3d
Butcher's half stall 9d
For every basket with butter, poultry, rabbits,
    game and wildfowl 2d
For every bushel of potatoes, turnips, carrots
    and other roots...................................... ½d

Fleetwood (Lancashire)
Where: Adelaide Street and Victoria Street
When: Tuesday and Friday all year round; plus Monday from May to October and Saturday from July to October
What: fruit, vegetables, clothes, tweed, shoes, souvenirs, pottery, curtaining, kitchen goods

The Fleetwood guide advertises this market as a 'world famous' attraction for holidaymakers in the Wyre district. The market is both indoor and outdoor, and has a total of 250 stalls and shop units. Country markets in the area are at Great Eccleston, where the Square sees the erection of 40 stalls on a Wednesday, and in Garstang High Street, which on Thursday accommodates 55 stalls supplying a wide range of interesting items. All these centres offer free parking and have numerous restaurants and pubs supplying lunch.

Fleetwood festivities start in May with the Maritime Festival running throughout the summer until September. Fleetwood hosts the International Folk Festival, a costume festival, a brass band competition, Morris dancing, a preserved-vehicle rally and a horticultural show. In addition there is a carnival and beauty contest.

Flint (Clwyd)
Where: Coast Road, adjacent to the station and Town Hall
When: Friday
What: about 60 stalls selling goods ranging from vegetables, plants, health foods and household goods to bric-à-brac

The Ship Hotel is situated right in the middle of the market area and there are several other pubs and cafés nearby. Flint was originally granted seven royal charters to operate a town market – despite this the market ceased to trade during the early 1900s, but was revived in 1950. Visitors to Flint market should take the opportunity of looking over the castle, which was built by Edward I after his defeat of the Welsh.

Folkestone (Kent)
Where: Lower Sandgate Road
When: Sunday
What: general retail goods

The market is held on the sea-front and there are many pubs, snack bars etc, nearby. Folkestone Carnival Week runs from 13 to 20 August, ending with a grand carnival procession. A week later the Rolls-Royce rally is held on The Leas.

Frome (Somerset)
Where: Cattle Market, Bridge Street
When: Wednesday (main market); Saturday (small market); and see below
What: food, clothes, fresh produce auction, and see below

Frome market is mentioned in the Domesday Book. The prosperity of Frome was founded in the fourteenth century on the cloth industry. Today it is primarily an agricultural centre with a large cattle market on Wednesday. The Frome Cheese Show, held on the third Wednesday in September, is the largest one-day agricultural show in the south-west. An antiques market is held in the Market Hall every Friday, and a craft market every Tuesday. There are several good pubs nearby.

Gainsborough (Lincolnshire)
Where: Market Place and Silver Street
When: Tuesday, Friday (indoor only), Saturday
What: fruit, vegetables, clothing, antiques, bric-à-brac, second-hand goods

The Domesday Book shows Gainsborough as a river trading centre with 800 inhabitants. By the Middle Ages it was an important wool centre, and it continued to grow until the coming of the railway in 1849, when its prosperity declined with the river traffic. The White Hart in Lord Street is recommended for lunch.

Galashiels (Borders)
Where: Currie Road
When: Friday
What: fresh fruit, vegetables, poultry, tinned goods, household
goods, fancies, textiles

The name 'Galashiels' is derived from the summer shelters or
'shielings' built by herdsmen on the banks of Gala Water. From the
herdsmen there came generations of spinners and weavers, and
today Galashiels is the centre of the Scottish woollen industry,
known internationally for the excellence of its tweeds which are of
prime interest to the visiting shopper. The Midsummer Fair was
licensed by charter in 1599 and survives today in the form of the
Braw (brave) Lads' Gathering at the end of June, when the locals
dress up to commemorate the slaying of a gang of English looters.
Recommended places for lunch are Abbotsford Arms Hotel,
Stirling Street; the Douglas Hotel and the Waverley Hotel, Channel
Street.

Glasgow
Where: The Barras
When: Saturday and Sunday
What: everything, including anchors. Specialities are second-hand
goods and clothes

The Barras is a very popular event in Glasgow and the stallholders
have their own language, Barrapatter. '22' is a good place to eat
near the market – it is recommended for its good food and
company.

Glastonbury (Somerset)
Where: the Cattle Market and the car-park adjoining
When: Tuesday
What: the market sells cattle, some produce and furniture. The
car-park market sells meat, cereals, fish, plants, junk and cheese –
in fact, a bit of everything

Glastonbury has industries in the sheepskin and leather trades. The Victorian market cross stands in the town centre, and the market is intriguing for the surprising mixture of goods on sale. Lunch is to be had at the George and Pilgrims, the Lamb Hotel and Rainbow's End, which serves good wholefood.

Major events in the calendar of Glastonbury are the Miracle Plays performed in July and August, and the Tor Fair or Fair of Glaston Twelve Hides, an ancient horse fair, held in the second week in September. The horse-trading has now become pony-trading, and the animals are sold in the cattle market.

Glossop (Derbyshire)
Where: Market Street off High Street West (indoor market behind the Town Hall)
When: Friday, Saturday
What: all kinds of food, clothing, hardware and fancy goods, a very good selection of cheeses and cooked meats, extremely cheap house-plants and exceptionally high quality greengrocery

The thirteenth Duke of Norfolk, the Lord of the Manor, built the Market Hall in 1844 and the railway station in 1847, and the Victorian era saw the expansion of an already flourishing wool and cloth trade. The Glossop Traders' Association celebrates a Victorian weekend in September, at which there are a steam- and traction-engine display, Dutch organs, vintage cars, a temperance band, a strong-man contest, street-sellers, Punch and Judy shows, brass bands, a tug-of-war, a pie-eating contest, Morris men and clog-dancers, a blacksmith's forge, music-hall entertainments, a flea-market, sideshows and children's games including whip-and-top and hoop-and-stick races. Shopkeepers, market stallholders and the public dress up in Victorian costumes, a prize being offered for the best one, and shop windows and goods on sale reflect the period spirit. In July there is a modern carnival with stalls run by local organizations and special events such as parachuting, giant Japanese wrestlers, open-air theatre, dancing majorettes, a Wild West show and hot-air balloons.

A good pub near the market is the Howard Arms in High Street East, which serves wholesome food at a reasonable price. The Tasty Bite opposite the car-park on Victoria Street offers quick snacks in clean surroundings, and children are welcome at any time of the day.

Gloucester
Where: Eastgate Street
When: Monday to Saturday
What: vegetables, fruit, meat, fish, cheese, bedding, curtaining, pet foods, plants and gardening equipment, shoes, bags

There is a cattle market in St Oswald's Road which sells livestock on Monday and Thursday. A general open market is held on the same site on Saturday morning. The pub recommended for lunch is the Bell and Gavel in the cattle-market.

Goole (North Humberside)
Where: Market Square
When: Wednesday, Friday, Saturday
What: general market

The Old George in the Market Square provides lunch.

Gosport (Hampshire)
Where: Clarence Road car-park, off High Street
When: Tuesday
What: fruit, vegetables, sweets, clothing, household goods

Bargain-hunters have a choice of three restaurants in the High Street – the Star, the Sunflower House (Chinese) and Crispins, a fish restaurant. Maritime Gosport holds a carnival and watersports in June, followed by the HMS *Sultan* Show, the Lee-on-Solent Show, and the HMS *Daedalus* Air Day in July, and a bus and car rally in August.

Grantham (Lincolnshire)
Where: Market Place and Westgate
When: Saturday
What: fruit, vegetables, plants, flowers, materials, china, shoes, clothes, harberdashery, ribbons, lace, toys, cosmetics, wallpapers, records, cakes, biscuits, and a very good cheese stall specializing in local cheeses

Grantham market was granted by charter of Richard III and was originally held on a Wednesday, later changed to Saturday. The site of the market is owned by Buckminster Estate, and the District Council pays £5,000 per annum for its lease. A stock market is held on Dysart Road on Thursday. The Angel and Royal, a 750-year-old hotel in the High Street not far from the market, is recommended for lunch; and the sandwiches at the Black Dog Inn on Watergate are good too.

Grantham has a mid-Lent fair held in the Market Place and in Westgate, which is one of the major shopping thoroughfares of the town. Showmen come from all over the country and put up sideshows and huge roundabouts in the streets. The fair lasts for three days, a Monday, Tuesday and Wednesday.

Gravesend (Kent)
Where: between High Street and Queen Street
When: covered market, Monday to Saturday; open market, Saturday
What: clothing of all kinds, jewellery, shoes, cosmetics, haberdashery, cards, records, eggs, fruit, vegetables, fish and sea-food, fishing tackle, flowers, plants, toiletries, curtains, curtaining, animal foodstuffs, kitchenware, confectionery, fancy goods, silk-flower arrangements, handbags, anoraks, jeans, tools, leather goods, lingerie, meat, key-cutting, perfume

One of the most colourful stalls in Gravesend market is Strongs fancy goods – Syd Strong has been in the market for more than fifty years. He is well known for tossing dinner services into the air and catching them without breakage, and has appeared on television with his son Gerald. The Reliance Fish Bar in Queen Street adjacent to the market is the place to eat in Gravesend: it is well patronized by the locals, and visitors on a tour of Gravesend are often given lunch there. Gravesend has a lively calendar of festivities; each year it holds a town regatta, the mayor's charity ball, a May Queen Parade and an Edwardian festival.

Great Yarmouth (Norfolk)
Where: Market Place, town centre
When: Monday to Saturday; additional stalls on Wednesday, Friday and Saturday in the summer season
What: fruit and vegetables, wet fish and sea-food, tripe, meat. Specialities are ice-creams, hot pies and peas, chips and other refreshments, especially during the holiday months

The Growler, in the market place, is a friendly pub with good food at reasonable prices – if you haven't already been tempted by the food on offer in the market. Yarmouth's annual fair is held on the weekend following Easter from 6 p.m. on Thursday through to Saturday night. It is held on the market place and also occupies two nearby car-parks.

Grimsby (South Humberside)
Where: Top Town Market Hall, at Friargate end of Riverhead shopping precinct
When: Tuesday, Friday, Saturday
What: general market selling most goods other than large items of furniture. The specialities are home-grown fruit and vegetables, flowers, bedding plants and house-plants

The open-air market traded on Friday in the market place but was superseded by the Top Town Market in 1976. The Salt Pot in the market sells good hot snacks including fish and chips. The Friar Tuck and Berni Inn are nearby, as is the Crest Motel, which is very good but not cheap. A fair visits Grimsby twice a year, in May and September.

Guernsey (Channel Islands)
Where: Market Place, St Peter Port
When: Monday to Saturday, half-day Thursday, but see below
What: meat, fish, fresh fruit, vegetables, flowers, Continental delicatessen, many local specialities, see below

Guernsey's daily market has a wide range of special foods, such as sausages, pâtés and quiches. The covered market in the French Halles also sells flowers and plants that holidaymakers can arrange to have sent home. But the main attraction is undoubtedly shellfish, with crabs, lobsters and crayfish fresh from the catch being cooked right there, at the customer's request. On Thursday afternoons from May to September, when the general market is closed, the open-air Old Guernsey Market takes place, offering local produce, including home-made cakes and jams, sold by people in traditional costume. Also on sale are crafts, including knitwear, jewellery, pottery and copperware, with reproductions of the original Guernsey can for carrying milk. There is a proliferation of eating places ranging from the superb cuisine of La Nautique on Quay Steps for a gastronomic holiday high-spot, to the Black Cat Bistro on Weighbridge, a handy place for waterfront browsers. Court's Wine Lodge in Le Marchant Street has more than forty realistically priced wines.

Guildford (Surrey)
Where: North Street
When: Friday, Saturday
What: fruit, vegetables, general provisions

At Slyfield Green near Guildford a cattle market is held on Tuesday and a general market on Wednesday. The Guildford Show is held on the first Saturday and Sunday in September.

Guisborough (Cleveland)
Where: both sides of Westgate, the town's main street
When: Thursday, Saturday
What: clothing, fruit, vegetables, hardware, fish, agricultural
supplies

The market is the heart of Guisborough and has been since the
Middle Ages. Take the opportunity to look at the ruins of the
Priory, first endowed in 1119, the medieval octagonal dovecote and
the market cross in cobbled Westgate. Three pubs are especially
recommended for home cooking and friendly atmosphere – the
Buck and the Three Fiddles in Westgate and the Fox in Bow Street.
Guisborough has a weekend festival at Easter.

Haddington (Lothian)
Where: East Fortune
When: Sunday
What: fresh produce, textiles, household goods, second-hand stalls,
clothing, hot food stalls

Haddington at present has no weekly town market, but the Sunday
market, which operates on a tarmac site in a rural area, is well
worth a visit if you have a car. Haddington has a town festival in
June and this includes a street fair and stalls.

Halesworth (Suffolk)
Where: Market Place
When: Wednesday
What: vegetables, fruit, flowers, fish, garden plants, clothes,
sometimes shoes and bric-à-brac, sweets, double-glazing, eggs,
cakes

On Wednesday morning there is also a WI market selling
home-made cakes, jams, plants etc in St Mary's Hall. A cattle
market and auction are held on alternate Wednesdays. Eat at the

Angel Hotel, where the fish is excellent, or at Warner's Wine Bar – good selection of wines, varied menu and friendly atmosphere.

Halifax (West Yorkshire)
Where: Market Street
When: Monday to Saturday
What: confectionery, footwear, groceries and provisions, fruit, flowers, vegetables, meat, clothing, drapery, millinery, toiletries, hardware, toys, fancy goods, books, newspapers, electrical goods, delicatessen, refreshments; fish in adjoining premises

Market traders used to set up stalls in the streets, or just stand there with baskets, until 1810 when all street trading was forbidden and traders moved to a new market place built of red brick on the site of the present Borough Market, which is still known today as the 'New Market', despite the fact that it was opened in 1896 by the Duke and Duchess of York (later King George V and Queen Mary). It is considered one of the finest market halls in the North of England, with a fine arcade on the east. Viewed from above, it gives an oriental impression with its central dome and surrounding towers embellished with ornamental finials. Shoppers can eat at the Portman and Pickles, adjoining the market.

This is not the only market worth visiting in Halifax: another outstanding building is the Halifax Piece Hall Market, built in 1779. The name comes from the cloth originally sold there, which was handwoven in thirty-yard lengths called 'pieces'. As well as general market stalls, there are forty craft shops in the colonnade. The Piece Hall Hotel and Restaurant offer reasonably priced food in quiet surroundings. This market is open on Friday and Saturday.

Harlow (Essex)
Where: Market Square
When: Tuesday, Thursday, Friday, Saturday
What: everything from greengrocery to dresses and toys

Harlow new town dates from 1947. Its master planner was Sir Frederick Gibberd, who said, 'Shopping is the only essential ingredient of a town centre and on its success much depends. The oldest form of shopping, a market, might be thought an anachronism in a new town, but it has brought life and bustle to the centre and traditional market trades not found in the shopping malls.' The market has 100 stalls and was opened in 1982. Nearby in Post Office Walk is a wine bar called Brasserie de la Poste, recommended for its lively atmosphere. The largest annual event in the town's calendar is the Harlow Town Show, a two-day affair held in August in the town park.

Harrogate (North Yorkshire)
Where: Market Hall
When: Monday to Saturday, half-day Wednesday
What: fruit, vegetables, meat, dairy produce, books, clothes, antiques, household goods

Visitors have poured into Harrogate for centuries to take the waters at its Sulphur Well, described by the Harrogate guidebook as 'most offensive to drink'. In 1841, after an attempt by a local hotelier to corner the market in sulphur water, an Act of Parliament was passed giving permission to develop Harrogate as a spa and to set up one or more markets to encourage the influx of tourists.

Restaurants near to the market are the Athenian Grill, Binns Café, Gresham Restaurant and Schofields Yorkshire Café, all in James Street.

Hatfield (Hertfordshire)
Where: Market Place
When: Wednesday, Saturday
What: wide range of general goods, including clothes, food and household items

The following extract comes from the *Book of Hatfield*:

> Hatfield's market days stretch back to 1226 when Henry III granted the bishops of Ely the rights to an annual four-day fair and a Thursday market. Standing on twelve timber stilts, the Market House was originally at the bottom of Fore Street, but was later moved to the top, opposite the church. Near the site remains a brick circle in the ground which was used as a cattle-auction ring. The church connection with the fair held on the feast of St Etheldreda added a word to the language: Etheldreda became Aldreda in Latin and was translated back into English as Audrey. Thus St Audrey became garbled into 'tawdry' and the new-coined adjective described the indifferent goods on sale; this also happened in other places which had a connection with the saint. The Hatfield market was an important one and in 1682 Lord Salisbury granted William Wright the profitable business of setting up the stalls and pens. Wright complained he was losing money because local residents traditionally set up stalls for tradespeople outside their homes and thus undermined his hoped-for monopoly. The annual fair lasted into this century, but by 1888 the market had vanished and was not re-established until 1957 in the New Town.

The White Hart is in Hatfield Market Place.

Hawick (Borders)
Where: The Auction Mart, Andrew Oliver & Sons, Weensland Road
When: general goods on Saturday; livestock sales on weekdays
What: general goods, clothing, fresh foodstuffs, children's goods, household goods, gardening produce, home baking, toys

The stalls in the general market vary from week to week. Andrew Oliver & Sons is the oldest livestock auction mart in Britain, having been founded in 1817 by an ancestor of the current generation of Olivers. The Farmer's Rest bar and restaurant is inside the market square compound, and is highly recommended for its good food.

The principal annual event in Hawick is the Common Riding, which is held in commemoration of a Scottish rout of invading English forces in 1514. Each year a cornet is elected along with his lass and an acting father. It is the cornet who presides over all the ceremonies, leading the acting father, the left and right-hand men (cornets from the previous two years) and a large number of Hawick horsemen on a series of weekly processions or rideouts around the various villages surrounding Hawick. The Common Riding culminates in two days of horse-racing on Hawick Moor. The townspeople come in droves to watch the racing, enjoy picnicking and looking for bargains on the various traders' stalls set up near the event. At the end of the Common Riding, the cornet hands the town flag (the banner) back to the provost of Hawick.

Hay-on-Wye (Powys)
Where: by the town clock and in the covered Buttermarket
When: Thursday
What: Linen, household, fresh produce, wholefood, excellent cheese stall, and first-class butcher's stall where the speciality is home-made sausages with all sorts of unusual ingredients, including oranges

Hay is a small Marches border town which was the scene of many a dispute between the English and Welsh. Its castle was built about 1200, but today the building is privately owned by Mr Richard Booth, a bookseller who has made Hay world famous for its antiquarian and second-hand books. There are about a dozen bookshops in the town catering for the general reader as well as the specialist. Some are open 364 days a year and during the summer they stay open into the evening.

Thursday is the day when the town really comes to life – the only day when outlying villages enjoy a bus service which brings people into town for the market. The colonnaded Buttermarket, built on the site of the old Market House in 1833, has recently been renovated, as has the sixteenth-century Bear Inn in the street of the same name. Hay is well provided with eating places steeped in history – the Black Lion is particularly recommended for its good food. At one time the town had no less than thirty-four pubs. Among those still going strong are the Wheatsheaf, the Blue Boar and the Crown Hotel. On market day they are licensed all day. Egon Ronay recommends the Granary for a wholefood lunch; and Lyons Corner House is very good value for families.

The cattle market is held on Mondays, and there is a breeders' fair in September with high-quality foals and Welsh cobs.

Haywards Heath (West Sussex)
Where: Market Place
When: Tuesday, Thursday, Sunday
What: cattle (Tuesday); general market with clothes, bric-à-brac and food (Thursday and Sunday)

Haywards Heath cattle market is one of the oldest in Sussex. The Dolphin Fair, organized by the local Round Table, is held every April. Nearby Burgess Hill has a market on Wednesday and Saturday selling clothes, bric-à-brac and food.

Helmsley (North Yorkshire)
Where: Old Market Place
When: Friday
What: general market goods, including fruit, vegetables, fish, clothes, leather goods, plants and sweets

In Anglo-Saxon times, the Helmsley market was held in the church graveyard. Later, however, the market cross was moved to the square, where it remains. The town was known as 'Elmeslac' in the Domesday Book (deriving from 'Vale of the Elms') and stands close to Rievaulx Abbey. Helmsley was granted a Borough charter in the late twelfth century, primarily through the influence of Robert Fursan, which suggests that the town was by then having success in trade. Certainly the Parliamentary forces considered Helmsley a

worthy target during the Civil War: the townspeople rallied under
the Royalist Sir Jordan Crosland, but Helmsley Castle, which
overlooks the Market Place, fell to the besiegers in 1644.

The richness of the town's past is reflected in many of the pubs
around the pretty Market Place. Eating-places of historical interest
include the Black Swan, the Feversham Arms and the Feathers
Hotel.

Helston (Cornwall)
Where: Coinage Hall Street; Penzance Road
When: Saturday (Coinage Hall Street); Monday (Penzance Road)
What: a general open-air market in Coinage Hall Street, selling a
wide range of goods; livestock only at Penzance Road

Helston's imposing Market House built of Cornish granite dates
from the first half of the nineteenth century. The town is chiefly
famous for its ancient and traditional Floral Dance held annually
on Flora Day, 8 May, when the town is gaily decorated with spring
flowers and greenery. The day starts with the Hel-en-tow ceremony,
which is a re-enactment of the slaying of the dragon; and a series of
dances, in the streets and in and out of shops, begins with the first at
7 a.m. (traditionally for serving-maids); another at 10 a.m. for
children (hundreds of local schoolchildren take part in this one); a
formal one at noon; and a final dance at 5 p.m. for people leaving
work.

Hemel Hempstead (Hertfordshire)
Where: Market Square, town centre
When: Thursday, Friday, Saturday, and see below
What: clothes, fruit and vegetables, shoes, toys, linen and numerous
other general goods

Hemel Hempstead has an antiques market on the Market Square
every Wednesday, which sells all kinds of items from junk and
bric-à-brac to collectors' pieces. There is an August Bank Holiday
carnival. Recommended for lunch is Snooks, opposite the

market-place – a Victorian-style restaurant named after Robert Snooks, a highwayman who was hanged in Boxmoor. It serves very substantial meals.

Henley-on-Thames (Oxfordshire)
Where: Upper Market Place
When: Thursday
What: vegetables, fruit, sweets, clothes, plants

The Market Place has a number of pubs and restaurants – the Argyll, Antico, the Victoria and Chef Peking. Henley is famous for its regatta held annually in early July, and also has a May Fair on the first Monday in May.

Hereford
Hereford has two main markets:

Where: Newmarket Street
When: Wednesday, Saturday
What: livestock and general (Wednesday); general (Saturday)

Where: Buttermarket
When: Monday to Saturday
What: country produce, general stalls

The Buttermarket, partially on the site of an ancient coaching inn called the Red Streak Tree, still has special stalls for country people to sell their produce alongside the commercial retailers.

During the second week of May the main streets of Hereford are transformed by the colourful May Fair, which was granted by ancient charter to the Bishop. At the Town Hall, by arrangement with the Town Clerk's Department, some of the best preserved English charters can be viewed. Meals are served at lunchtime in the Booth Hall Hotel, East Street; Hop Pole and Merton Hotel, Commercial Road; Kerry Arms, Commercial Square; and Saxty's Wine Bar, Widemarsh Street.

Hexham (Northumberland)
Where: Market Place
When: Tuesday
What: a general market with food, clothes, toys, plants, handbags

You can eat in the Market Place at the Albany Café and in Market Street at the Heart of All England Inn. Hexham has an annual fair in August.

High Wycombe (Buckinghamshire)
Where: High Street, Guildhall, Market Square
When: Tuesday, Friday, Saturday
What: a very wide variety of goods; especially good cheese

In March there is the Wycombe Arts Festival, which features concerts, plays and exhibitions of paintings. On the last Thursday in May is the mayor-making ceremony: the new mayor of High Wycombe and all the members of the council are publicly weighed, as are the outgoing mayor and councillors. The weights are recorded and compared at the end of each year's office. If the mayor has put on weight, he is jeered by the crowd for having grown fat at the expense of the ratepayers. On the first Saturday in September is the Wycombe Show, an agricultural show held at Wycombe Rye. There are exhibitions of livestock, horticulture, crafts and steam engines, to the accompaniment of music from massed brass bands.

Hitchin (Hertfordshire)
Where: adjacent to St Mary's Square
When: Tuesday, Saturday, Bank Holidays
What: wide range of goods including food, bags, wool, clothing, household goods, and see below

The market is situated in a very picturesque spot next to St Mary's Church, the largest in Hertfordshire and a fine example of fifteenth-century craftsmanship. The area is dense with medieval houses, inns and almshouses. On Thursdays the market is devoted to antiques, bric-à-brac, second-hand stalls and collectors' items. The West Alley antique and collectors' market is open on Tuesday, Saturday and Bank Holidays and also features stalls selling local crafts. The Sun Hotel in Sun Street is recommended for its good, reasonably priced carvery.

Hoddesdon (Hertfordshire)
Where: High Street
When: Wednesday
What: fruit, vegetables, tinned goods, fabrics, clothes, household goods

In 1253 Richard de Boxe was granted a charter by Henry III to hold a market on Thursday each week at Hoddesdon and an annual fair on the Feast of St Martin. In 1560 a further charter was granted by Queen Elizabeth, which established a grammar school in Hoddesdon and granted the tolls of a weekly market and a fair on the Feast of St Peter for the maintenance of the school. This market petered out, and the present-day market was started by a Mr Bridgman in 1886.

In the High Street pubs serving lunch are the White Swan, the Salisbury Arms and the Golden Lion, and just across from the clock-tower is the Bell.

A funfair is held at Pound Close at the end of June/beginning of July. The Hoddesdon carnival takes place on the second Saturday in September, the procession ending in the neighbouring district of Broxbourne in a fête at Deaconsfield.

Holywell (Clwyd)
Where: main car-park, town centre
When: Thursday
What: a small market, but offering plenty of variety – clothes, china, fish, confectionery, jewellery, health foods, eggs, toys, pet foods

A market charter was first granted in the eighteenth century to Sir John Egerton, but it fell into disuse. In 1977 a market was started up again by popular demand and there are plans to extend it with the redevelopment of Holywell. Several catering establishments are nearby.

Honiton (Devon)
Where: street market in High Street; cattle market in Silver Street
When: street market on Tuesday and Saturday; cattle market on Tuesday
What: the street market sells 'everything'

The earliest reference to a fair in the town dates from 1221, when a fair was held on All Hallows Day. In 1247 the date of the fair was changed to St Margaret's Day, 20 July, where it has remained ever since. The fair is opened by the town crier with a ceremony which has been in use for many centuries, though its origin is unknown. The ceremony is accompanied by the custom of throwing hot pennies to the assembled children.

The Angel Hotel in the High Street is recommended for lunch: in 1605 it was already being referred to as 'an old established inn'. Today it has RAC and AA stars and is a member of Les Routiers.

Horsham (West Sussex)
Where: Carfax
When: Saturday
What: wide variety of goods, including greengrocery

Horsham Central Market is privately owned. It was established in 1933 by Mr Alfred Durrant on the ground behind the furniture shop he owned, and where his father before him had lived over the top of the shop. The market is on what was originally the family's garden and has been trading now without a break for fifty-four years. When Alfred died, his son Douglas took over. When he died in 1977

Douglas's widow took over the market and ran it until 1984, when her son William took over. There are stalls of various trades and the atmosphere is that of a family party. The greengrocer's family has been there for fifty-three years, and Mrs Alice Lovett, who was there at the beginning, still serves on the stall. They started selling bunches of flowers and plants, and then went into greengrocery and fruit. Unfortunately this area is to be redeveloped in the next few years and unless the market can be relocated it will be the end of an era for the Durrant family.

For lunch Mrs Durrant recommends the King's Head Hotel, Carfax, an old coaching inn, which has reasonable prices and is full of character.

Huddersfield (West Yorkshire)
Where: Brook Street
When: Monday, Thursday
What: fruit, vegetables, provisions, clothes. Speciality: textiles, and see below

Huddersfield is a town built on the textile industry and its fine wool worsteds are a speciality of the market. Spinning and weaving were cottage crafts here for centuries until the textile mills were built about 200 years ago, powered first by water and then by steam. The development of the town was owed largely to one family, the Ramsdens, who were responsible for gaining royal assent to hold a market and for building the Cloth Hall, Ramsden Canal and the railway. The Brook St Market Hall with its cast-iron work, glazed walls and elaborate detailing dates from 1887 and originally served as a wholesale market. It has recently been sensitively restored and converted to a general market. A bric-à-brac market is held here on Tuesdays. There is also a daily market (half-day Wednesday) at Market Hall, Princess Alexandra Walk.

Recommended for lunch is the George Hotel, St George's Square. A café and mobile snack bars are to be found in the open market.

Hull (Humberside)
Where: King Street (open market); North Churchside (covered market)
When: Tuesday, Friday, Saturday (open market); Monday to Saturday (covered market)
What: the open market sells absolutely everything, while the covered market concentrates mainly on fruit, vegetables, meat, fish and other provisions

Hull market is famous for an incident that took place on 4 February 1806. George Gowthorpe of Patrington, a village about fifteen miles east of Hull, sold his wife in the market-place for twenty guineas and delivered her in a halter to a Mr Houseman.

Pubs to have lunch in are the Cellar Bar, the Waterfront Hotel, Dagger Lane, and the Old Warehouse, which is recommended for its good atmosphere.

Hull Fair is claimed by the city to be the biggest fair in Britain and the biggest movable funfair in Europe. It takes place at Walton Street fairground, usually starting on the Saturday nearest 11 October, and lasts a week.

Hunstanton (Norfolk)
Where: Central Car-Park (small market); Town Front (main market)
When: small market, Wednesday; main market, Sunday
What: a general selection of goods is sold, including some second-hand goods

Huntingdon (Cambridgeshire)
Where: Market Hall
When: Saturday
What: fruit, vegetables, clothes, books, cheese, eggs, jewellery, charity stall

Oliver Cromwell was born and educated in Huntingdon, and the Falcon Inn in Huntingdon Market Square was his headquarters during the Civil War. The Falcon and the Market Inn both serve lunches. Huntingdon has an annual carnival, usually held in the third week in June. There is a raft race on the river, a football match and a drama competition, besides a parade and a fête on the Saturday.

Huntly (Grampian)
Where: Aberdeen Road
When: Wednesday
What: cattle, sheep, and local products such as shortbread and saddlery

The Huntly mart has its own catering facilities and the adjacent Battlehill Hotel offers a full meals service. The main fairs held in Huntly are the Huntly Gala (end of June) and the Flower Show (end of August).

Ilkeston (Derbyshire)
Where: Market Place
When: Thursday, Saturday
What: meat, fruit, vegetables, fish, cheeses, fabrics, clothing, lace

Ilkeston was awarded a charter in 1252, permitting a weekly market and an annual fair which is still held in October each year, when the town centre is closed to traffic and the Market Place becomes a brilliantly lit funfair with stalls for confectionery, toys and local produce. Ilkeston is a centre of the textile industry and the market town for the Erewash Valley. Several pubs round the Market Square are noted for their real ale.

Inverness (Highland)
Where: Craig Road
When: Tuesday, Wednesday, Friday
What: fruit, vegetables, meat, home-made produce, clothes, fabrics, household goods

Ipswich

In the nineteenth century a new market was opened in Inverness, which made it the centre of the Highland sheep and wool trade. The Croft Restaurant is recommended for a market lunch. In Dores Road there is a workshop where you can watch spinning and the weaving of tartan and tweed. Inverness's famous annual event is the Highland Games in July and August.

Ipswich (Suffolk)
Where: Crown Street, town centre
When: Tuesday, Friday, Saturday
What: fruit and vegetables, meat and meat products, fresh fish, bread, cheese, frozen foods, tinned foods, wholefoods, confectionery, cakes, pet foods, snacks, flowers and plants, toiletries, eggs, engraving, woollens, lingerie, underwear, fashions, working clothes, foul-weather gear, footwear, children's clothes, haberdashery, wool, dress materials, curtains, seat covers, jewellery, greetings cards, key-cutting, showers, double-glazing

The Town House, Crown Street is recommended for lunch. The Ancient House in the Buttermarket is emblazoned with the coat-of-arms of Charles II and a fifteenth-century extravaganza of ornate plasterwork.

Kendal (Cumbria)
Where: Market Hall and Market Place, town centre
When: Monday (bric-à-brac), Wednesday and Saturday
What: the general market sells fabrics, local produce and household goods. The sexy undies stall generates a special interest

Kendal grew up as the main market town of Westmorland with the wool industry initially forming the main basis for trade. The Monday bric-à-brac and collectors' market offers items of interest to the serious collector and the fancier of unusual bits and pieces. Among its specialities are military souvenirs, guns, stamps and woodworking and other craft tools from bygone times. Stallholders are as interested in buying from their customers as they are in selling to them. The Kendal Gathering is held in August and September and features concerts and other entertainments culminating in a grand torchlight procession. The Fleece Inn is recommended for lunch, its hot curries and attractive bar staff coming in for equal amounts of praise.

Keswick (Cumbria)
Where: Market Square
When: Saturday
What: fruit, vegetables, fresh pork, chicken, fish, cheeses, clothes, plants, bulbs, linen, bric-à-brac, hardware

Keswick's market charter was granted in the thirteenth century. The Market Place is dominated by the Moot Hall which until recently housed a food market for local produce: it is now an information centre for the surrounding Lakeland district. In the Square are several places to eat including the Skiddaw Hotel, the Kings Arms and the Golden Lion. All provide reasonably priced snacks and more substantial Cumbrian fare. Keswick holds an annual Victorian market on the second weekend in December.

Kettering (Northamptonshire)
Where: Sheep Street
When: Wednesday, Friday, Saturday
What: on Wednesday antiques; Friday and Saturday general goods on 70 stalls, including fresh provisions, fruit and vegetables, footwear, knitwear, clothes, leather goods, flowers

The charter to hold a market at Kettering was granted in 1227 by Henry III to the Abbot of Peterborough and his monks. With the Dissolution of the Monasteries, ownership passed to the Crown, then to the Lords of the Manor, the Watsons of Rockingham Castle and the Montagus of Boughton House. Today's Lords of the Manor are Mr Michael Watson of Rockingham Castle and the Duke of

Buccleuch of Boughton House, but the running of the market has been in the hands of the corporation since the 1880s. In 1977 a medieval market celebrated 750 years of market trading in Kettering and proved so popular that it has been repeated every year since. The market florist who stands at the front of the market claims his family has traded there for 300 years without a break. The George and the Royal Hotel offer refreshment nearby; both have varied menus to suit all pockets.

King's Lynn (Norfolk)
Where: Tuesday Market Place, Saturday Market Place
When: Tuesday, Friday (Tuesday Market Place); Saturday (Saturday Market Place)
What: Tuesday – clothing, edibles (fish, fruit, vegetables, meat etc), household goods, drapery, haberdashery, wool, materials, curtains, leisure/gifts, horticulture, handbags, purses, footwear, hardware, glazing, electrical and cycle accessories, bric-à-brac, pet foods, miscellaneous. There are 150 stalls. Friday – forty-one traders in clothing, edibles, toys, fancy goods, jewellery, bags, purses, footwear, household goods, hardware, horticulture and pet foods. Saturday – thirty-seven traders in edibles, clothing, toys, fancy goods, jewellery, horticulture, bric-à-brac, cycle accessories, bags, purses, wool and pet foods

The Tuesday market is dominated by clothing, the Saturday market by food. The Saturday market started in 1453 and the Tuesday market was established during the reign of Richard I. The Tuesday market, known as the Forum Martic, was also the site of civic punishments: in 1436 forty-three witches were burned at the stake, sixty-three people were hanged for shop lifting, and a maidservant was burned to death for murdering her mistress. There was a whipping post at which children were whipped for disobedience, and stocks which were used to punish anyone who broke the king's peace. A new set of stocks was commissioned as late as 1890 from Robert Mathew, a blacksmith, who placed them outside his home for his own pleasure. The Lynn assembly informed him that if he did not remove them to the Tuesday Market Place, he would be the first to try them out. The story has it that he removed them at 1 a.m. that very morning.

In 1309 a fair was set up in King's Lynn. The largest in all England at that time, it ran for six weeks and attracted most of Norfolk's craftsmen and skilled manufacturers, who brought goods they had made. Usually the majority of them sold out within three weeks, but not to local people, who knew they could get the same goods 15 per cent cheaper in the shops! To open the fair, the mayor, aldermen and common council dressed in scarlet and met at the Guildhall to elect twenty freemen from the burgesses. These young men were each given a parchment with a pendant seal. At one o'clock they set off for the Tuesday Market Place, where a proclamation was read and the fair declared open. At the end of the mart it was the practice for the traders to give the townspeople a lamp or a drinking fountain.

Two months after the annual mart a cheese fair was held, at which the mayor was presented with some of Lynn's own cheese. This fair lasted two days and sold cheese, potatoes and onions. Sadly the fair had left Lynn and moved to Norwich by 1900, owing to Lynn's decline in importance.

The charter on which today's markets are based was granted by Henry VIII in 1529. However, markets were a feature of the town long before that time and date back at least to 1205 and the charter of King John. The Lynn Mart, held annually on St Valentine's Day in the Tuesday Market Place, dates from 1529. Many of today's stallholders have traded for more than twenty years. One of their most popular and unusual specialities is samphire, a seaweed harvested from the Norfolk marshes. It is traditionally served lightly boiled, liberally seasoned with vinegar and accompanied by brown bread and butter.

Offering lunch near the Tuesday Market Place are the Mayden's Head, the Duke's Head, the Globe and the Woolpack. Saturday Market Place has Wenn's Charterhouse Bistro.

Kingston-upon-Thames (Surrey)
Kingston-upon-Thames has two markets:

Where: Market Square
When: Monday to Saturday (early closing on Wednesday)
What: fruit and vegetables

Where: Fairfield Road
When: Monday morning
What: a general market

The town's market charter dates from 1242. Recently, the council has organized a fair on the first Bank Holiday in May, during which antiques are sold in the Market Square instead of the usual fruit and vegetables, and there are fireworks in the evening. The Druids pub serves lunch.

Kirkby (Merseyside)
Where: St Chad's Parade
When: Tuesday, Saturday
What: meat, fish, dairy produce, bread, cakes, biscuits, grocery, pet food, curtains, bed-linen, clothes, fruit, vegetables, household goods, flowers, stationery, carpets, furniture, wool, shoes, bags, home-brew (Saturday only), toiletries, haberdashery, picture-frames, toys, records, jewellery, second-hand goods, electrical goods, fur fabric, paperback books, pottery, papers and magazines, sports equipment and sportswear, frozen foods, cosmetics, gardening equipment and plants, sweets, sheepskin, fur and leather coats, ice-creams, mirrors and blinds

Kirkby Lonsdale (Cumbria)
Where: Market Square
When: Thursday
What: About twenty stalls selling local produce, clothes and other goods

Kirkbymoorside (North Yorkshire)
Where: Market Place
When: Wednesday
What: general market, including fruit, vegetables, fish, leather goods and clothing

The steep, partly cobbled Market Place in Kirkbymoorside, on the edge of the North York Moors, has three old hotels at its side: the King's Head, the George and Dragon, and the Black Swan.

Kirkwall (Orkney)
Where: Market Place
When: Monday
What: local produce: meat, poultry, eggs, Orkney cheese, soft farm cheese, oatcakes, shellfish, fresh fish, locally smoked salmon and kippers, bread, Orkney fudge

High tea is an Orkney tradition and consists of a main dish, perhaps fish, then home-baked scones, cakes and shortbread. Recommended for such a feast is the Albert Hotel, Mounthoolie Place. Visitors should also look out for details of WI sales of work and coffee evenings where the home-baking stalls enjoy a brisk trade. There are two malt-producing distilleries, at Highland Park and Scapa, both near Orkney's capital Kirkwall. The Boardhouse Mill at Birdsay is worth a visit – it is a watermill and grinds oats and wheat, which can be bought on the premises. The Ba' game, a sort of rugby football, is played on Christmas Day and New Year's Day – an Orkney custom dating from Viking times.

Knaresborough (North Yorkshire)
Where: Market place
When: Wednesday
What: provisions and general goods

Markets have been held in Knaresborough since the time of Alfred the Great. Knaresborough open-air market, busy and thriving, is one of the most famous in the north of England. In addition to the general Wednesday market, which draws visitors from miles around, there is a Monday cattle market. The market rights were purchased for the town in 1888 for the sum of £870. One of the many ancient buildings in the Market Place is reputedly the oldest chemist's shop in England, established as a pharmacy in 1720, during the reign of King George I, though it was a dwelling house for hundreds of years before this.

The Knaresborough Bed Race has been a major attraction now for twenty years. Each year sees the course completed in record time by a record number of beds – fifty-five have been known to enter. The race is held in the grounds of Conyngham Hall and for the spectators – who number up to 60,000 – the highlight is watching the beds' crews plough full tilt through the River Nidd, often with disastrous results for the furniture.

The most delicious fish and chips are to be eaten at Aragon Fisheries, Iles Lane.

Knighton (Powys)
Where: Clock Tower
When: Thursday
What: a very attractive and intimate market – it has only about 10 stalls which sell a variety of items

The nineteenth-century Clock Tower stands on the site of the Town Hall, and it is around this that the traders set up their stalls. Knighton market used to sell livestock (there is now a separate sheep and cattle market) and even wives, the last two recorded instances of wife-selling being in 1851 and 1854. Each of the women went for one shilling.

Knutsford (Cheshire)
Where: Silkmill Street
When: Friday, Saturday
What: a general market with fruit, vegetables, cheese, poultry, clothes, plants and flowers

Knutsford is named after King Canute (or Knut), who is supposed to have forded the lily stream between what are now Over Knutsford and Nether Knutsford. The right to hold a Saturday market and fairs on the feast day and morrow of Saints Peter and Paul was derived from a royal charter granted to William de Tabley by Edward I in 1292; a charter of 1332 granted the right to hold a fair on the eve, feast day and morrow of Saints Simon and Jude. Knutsford also has a Thursday cattle market, and on every second Wednesday there is a sale of implements. Today Knutsford is famous for its Royal May Day celebrations, when a procession through the town features Highwayman Higgins, Jack-in-the-Garden and the Royal May Queen. The fair is a traditional one with no machine-driven attractions. There is a maypole and the guidebook mentions 'devices laid out in vari-coloured sand', whatever these might be.

Places to eat near the market are the Freemasons Arms, Silkmill Street; in King Street, the Rose and Crown, Sir Frederick's and Cross Keys; and in Princess Street, the Royal George and King's Wine Bar.

Lampeter (Dyfed)
Where: the Common, between Harford Row and Victoria Terrace
When: alternate Tuesdays
What: fruit, clothing, meat, vegetables, ironmongery and many interesting second-hand stalls

Lampeter market has been held since 1284. The Royal Oak, Black Lion and Castle are all pubs in the High Street. The Rhys Thomas James Eisteddfod is held in August.

Lanark (Strathclyde)
Where: Ladyacre Road and Hyndford Road
When: Monday
What: an auction market selling all kinds of animals from cows to rabbits. Fruit, vegetables, plants, cheese and eggs are also on sale

Lanark is the chief market town of the Clydesdale district and its livestock market is one of the largest in Scotland. It is believed that Lanark received its charter in 1140. The medieval town was one of the four burghs of Scotland where the Standard Weights were kept. A good time to visit Lanark is during Lanimer Week in June. The name 'Lanimers' is derived from Land Marches, stones marking the burgh boundaries in medieval times. Hundreds of people turn out on the Monday of Lanimer Week for the Perambulation of the Marches, probably an annual event since 1140, when the March Stones are inspected. The two-hour walk ends with the Shifting of the Standard, when the burgh standard is passed from the old to the new Lord Cornet for safe-keeping until the following year. The highlight of the week comes on the Thursday with the Lanimer Day Carnival.

Lancaster
Where: Common Garden Street; also Church Street
When: main market, – Monday, Tuesday, Thursday, Friday and Saturday; Church Street market, – Wednesday and Saturday
What: the main market has 75 stalls and 20 antique and craft stalls. The 75 general stalls sell fresh and cooked meat, fish, fruit and vegetables, groceries, farm produce, garden produce, frozen foods, bakery, confectionery, delicatessen goods, health foods, brewing requisites, snacks, clothing, footwear, textiles, household textiles, wools and accessories, sewing machines, floor coverings, household goods, foam rubber, crockery and glassware, DIY goods, electrical goods, gas appliances, bags and leather goods, basketware, Indian crafts, fancy goods, bric-à-brac, records, video equipment, books, stationery, toys, jewellery, engraving, greetings cards, tobacconist goods, hairdressing goods and pets' requisites. Church Street market sells fruit, vegetables and flowers

Lancaster is proud of its nineteenth-century Market Hall, which is closely bound up with the history of the city. One of the most picturesque markets in Lancashire, it is a popular tourist attraction, and has a multi-span pitched roof with glass lantern lights on ornamental cast-iron columns. Lancaster also offers an attractive pedestrian shopping precinct and, on Wednesday and Saturday, a thriving outdoor vegetable market comprising 20 stalls.

The mural above the Market Hall entrance, called 'The Fortress on the Lune', commemorates the historical past of Lancaster and depicts a knight defending the foundation charter of the city, which was granted in 1193. It also shows the Celtic Cross of the original settlers and a crossroads representing Horseshoe Corner, where a horseshoe is buried, commemorating the horse fairs. Trade with the West Indies is represented by sugar-loaves, cotton bales and rum barrels. Rolls of oilcloth and linoleum remind the townsfolk that their manufacture greatly increased the city's prosperity from about 1845, while the ancient spinning and weaving industries of Lancaster make their appearance in the form of spinning machinery, cogwheels, cones of thread, and sheep.

Snacks are available in the market place and there are plenty of pubs and restaurants nearby.

Launceston (Cornwall)
Where: Race Hill
When: Saturday
What: vegetables, fruit, produce, shoes, clothes, animals in the main market, and fish on the lower ground floor of the Market Hall

Launceston is the ancient capital of Cornwall, and in Saxon times it was the home of the royal mint. It is the market town for the wide area between Bodmin Moor and Dartmoor. There is an agricultural show on the third Thursday in July and St Leonard's Fair on the third Tuesday in November. The Newmarket Inn is recommended for its good food.

Ledbury (Hereford and Worcester)
Where: Market House, High Street
When: Tuesday, Saturday morning
What: pet foods, clothes, bric-à-brac and cheese. Locally made cheese is a speciality, available on Saturday mornings only

A market charter was obtained for Ledbury in about 1122 by the bishop of Hereford, who had a formal wedge-shaped market laid out below the informal Saxon one. Two rows of stalls were also erected on market days and fair days in High Street and Bye Street. These were later replaced with permanent structures on Middle Row and Shop Row. Market House was built in the early seventeenth century as a corn market; the upper floor is now used as a meeting hall but the ground floor is still used as an open market. Take a look at the old notices still displayed in this area and note the differences in style of timber framing used on the various elevations.

Try the Market Place Coffee Shop for lunch or the Prince of Wales in Church Lane. Ledbury has a hop fair on the first Monday and Tuesday in October.

Leeds (West Yorkshire)
Where: Tuesday
When: Kirkgate Hall
What: a huge variety in shops and on stalls. Look out particularly for woollen cloth

It is not known when a market was first held in Leeds, but one was first recorded in 1626, when it was held on Mondays in a street called Briggate. In those days Leeds was already famous for its woven materials, and the cloth market on the bridge was described as 'the life not of this town alone, but these parts of England'. The chapel bell was rung to signal the end of cloth trading, when the market stalls were given over to drapers and shoemakers. In the eighteenth century cloth halls were built to house this growing trade. Other markets in Briggate sold corn, fruit, fish, meat, milk cows, wool, horses and pigs. A market cross in the form of a shelter was erected in 1626 to protect the farmers' wives and daughters from the elements while they sold butter and eggs. To stop unfair trading by 'forestallers', it was decreed that no corn should be sold until the market bell had been rung at 10 a.m. Bells were still being rung in the Corn Exchange as late as 1939, though their purpose by then was to remind the dealers not to miss their trains home.

By the mid-nineteenth century, the area around Briggate had become so congested that new markets were built. Today's Kirkgate Market Hall dates from 1904 – an imposing five-storey stone building adorned with carvings, domes and minarets and with marble pillars between the outside shops. Inside the walls are of glazed brickwork; four balconies surrounding the hall house shops and the hall stalls. At the time of writing the future of this splendid building is in dispute: there have been moves to demolish it to make way for a bus station and car-parks, but local feeling is strongly in favour of preserving it as it is.

The Corn Exchange is another building of note – this was opened in 1863, and is an oval-shaped stone building covered by a domed roof in one span which has glass in it to light the factors' market. The cellarage beneath it is given over to the wine and spirit business.

The shopper will also be intrigued by the city's Victorian shopping arcades, which are built like the naves of churches with lofty glazed roofs.

Leicester
Where: two markets, both in the city centre
When: outdoor market, Monday to Friday; covered market, Tuesday to Saturday
What: the large outdoor market sells second-hand goods as well as fruit, vegetables and clothes. The indoor market sells dairy products, meat, fish, poultry, childrens' clothes, shoes and other items

The Leicester market has long been in existence: there is documentation of Henry III's directive which moved the town's fifteen-day fair, celebrating the feast of the Purification, from June to February. A festival with a theme is now held annually in August. (The theme for 1987, for instance, was Simon De Montfort.)

Leighton Buzzard (Bedfordshire)
Where: along both sides of the High Street
When: Tuesday, Saturday
What: vegetables, fruit, telephones, electrical goods, tools, clothes, foam, shoes, snacks, pet goods, crockery, make-up, household goods, linen, cards, stationery, hardware, records

The Golden Bell in Church Square is recommended for good food, reasonable prices and a friendly atmosphere. Leighton Buzzard already had a weekly market by the time of the Domesday Book. The town has an annual marathon and an annual carnival.

Leominster (Hereford and Worcester)
Where: Friday
When: Corn Square
What: assorted stalls offering linen, clothes, meat, fish, cheese, confectionery, plants, shoes

Lewes (East Sussex)
Where: Market Tower, High Street
When: Tuesday morning
What: fruit, vegetables, Women's Institute home produce

The WI stalls in this attractive small market specialize in anything home-grown or handmade. The market tower stands on the site of the original Lewes market and was built to house the town bell, Gabriel, which was cast in the sixteenth century and is still rung on special occasions. The Lewes Arms in Fisher Street nearby serves good food and there are plenty of attractive shops within browsing distance selling antiques, pottery and crafts. The Felix Gallery in Sun Street sells antique and collectable cats. There is a raft race in May and Bonfire Night is always celebrated on 5 November unless it falls on a Sunday.

In nearby Southover a general and cattle market is held in Gardiner Street on Monday and Friday and visitors to this market can lunch at the King's Head in Southover High Street.

Leysdown (Kent)
Where: sea-front car-park
When: Sunday
What: a general market with emphasis on gifts and novelties

Lichfield (Staffordshire)
Where: Market Square
When: Friday, Saturday
What: food, vegetables, clothes, pottery, household goods, etc

The provision for a Friday market belongs to a charter signed by Richard I in 1189. The Saturday market has been held for only a few years, although provision for this was granted in 1623. There is a cattle market on Monday at Smithfield Market on Greenhill.

Lichfield Shrovetide Fair is held in the Market Square on Shrove Tuesday. It is opened with a traditional ceremony featuring a procession of mayor, sheriff, sword and mace bearers, charter trustees and civic officials who walk from the Guildhall to the Market Square. There the town crier proclaims that the fair is legally open for 'the sale of all goods, wares and vendible commodities whatsoever, paying the usual stallages, pick-idges, customs and duties for the same, and not using any fraud or deceit in buying or selling any unwholesome provisions whatsoever.' He then announces that: 'The court of Pie Powder (see page 10) will be held in the Guildhall for the redressing of all grievances or complaints that shall happen to arise during the time of the fair.'

The Pie Powder court is no longer held, but visitors can watch a pancake race in Market Street while the civic procession returns to the Guildhall to partake of refreshments, including simnel cake. Simnel cake is said to have its origins in a dispute between a man called Simon and his wife Nell, who argued as to whether a plum pudding should be boiled or baked. As they could not agree, it was both boiled and baked, producing the 'sim-nel'.

The convening of two ancient courts is celebrated in Lichfield. St George's Court, held on St George's Day, 23 April, at the Guildhall, recalls the settlement by fines of nuisance, neglect and trespass, and is attended by specially appointed high constables, dozeners, pinners and ale-tasters. The Court of Arraye is held on Whit Monday (Spring Bank Holiday Monday) also at the Guildhall; it was convened by the bailiffs to assess the defences of the town, including the arms and armour of its inhabitants. On the same day the Spring Festival, which has its origins in pagan worship, is held on the Greenhill. The mayor crowns the Bower Queen and during the afternoon there are various events, sports and attractions held in Beacon Park, while a market is held throughout the day in Market Street.

The Sheriff's Ride takes place around the city boundaries (about twenty-two miles) as near to 8 September as possible. This custom dates from Queen Mary's charter in 1553, when Lichfield was separated from Staffordshire and made a county in its own right. The ride is punctuated with stops for refreshments.

The birthday of Dr Johnson, who was born in Lichfield, is celebrated on the nearest Saturday to 18 September with a ceremony in Market Square, and hymns and a candlelit supper in the Guildhall with steak and kidney pudding, ale, punch and clay pipes.

You can lunch at St Mary's in Market Square or at the Corn Exchange; also at the Acorn in Tamworth Street and the Scales in Market Street.

Lincoln
Where: Sincil Street, off High Street
When: daily, but the best days are Thursday, Friday, Saturday
What: fruit, vegetables, household goods; especially noted for a wide range of cheeses and fresh fish

Lincoln is twinned with Neustadt an der Weinstrasse in Germany and the close links between the two towns have been the inspiration for the Christmas Market held every year from 12 to 15 December in Bailgate, with its half-timbered houses and cobbled streets in the shadow of the magnificent cathedral. The three-day festival lasts until 9.30 in the evenings and features German wine-tasting, *glühwein* and *würstchen* as well as hot chestnuts and mince pies. Toy stalls, church bells, Christmas trees, charcoal fires and carol-singing children are other attractions. The Green Dragon in Broadgate, the Witch and Wardrobe in Waterside and High Bridge Café, Highbridge, are all recommended for lunch.

Littlehampton (West Sussex)
Where: Surrey Street
When: Friday, Saturday, Sunday
What: fruit, vegetables, meat, eggs, cheese, pet foods, shoes, clothing, bric-à-brac, sheepskins, jewellery, toys, games, tools, cards, cakes, sweets, books, fish, hardware, socks, electrical goods

There is an excellent café in River Road with a takeaway service available. It is cheap and friendly with good home cooking.

Liverpool
Liverpool has four retail markets as well as a wholesale fruit, vegetable and flower market (six mornings a week at Edge Lane), a wholesale meat market (five mornings a week at Prescott Road) and a wholesale fish and poultry market (six mornings a week, next to the meat market).
    The central retail markets are:

St John's Market Hall, adjoining St John's Centre shopping precinct, open six days a week, selling foodstuffs and manufactured goods
Broadway Market, Broad Lane, Norris Green, selling food and manufactured goods five and a half days a week (half-day Wednesday)
St Martin's Market Hall, Great Homer Street, selling second-hand goods, clothing and new goods five and a half days a week (half-day Wednesday)
Monument Place Open Market, London Road, with 16 stalls selling manufactured goods on Thursday, Friday and Saturday

Liverpool's markets had their beginnings in King John's charter of 1207. In 1773 the market rights were purchased from the Molyneux family by the Corporation. St John's Market (1822), Cazeneau Street's wholesale fruit market (1859) and the adjoining vegetable market (1866) were landmarks in the development of Liverpool's growing market system. The North Markets at Cazeneau Street are on the route from the farmlands and market gardens of south-west Lancashire and take their atmosphere from the growers, while St John's Market has closer connections with the port. During the Second World War the North Markets were bombed twice and the buildings destroyed. Traders carried on for twenty-five years in tin shacks and in the open air, waiting for new accommodation. 1970 was also the year of the opening of the new St John's Market. All Liverpool's markets have nearby pubs.

Llandrindod Wells (Powys)
Where: Railway Goods Yard
When: Friday
What: general – produce, clothing etc.

The town of Llandrindod Wells is little more than a century old – a Victorian spa – and it celebrates with a Victorian festival every September. The extravaganza includes Victorian shopwindow displays, period costumes, a torchlight procession, music-hall acts, a steam rally, street theatre, jugglers, fire-eaters, unicyclists, horses and carriages for hire, tea-dances, bandstand concerts and performances of Gilbert and Sullivan. Visitors can also take the waters, should they feel the need of a sulphurous purgative which 'when thrown on hot iron emits a blue flame and smells like brimstone' and 'changes silver leaves in less than five minutes to a fine gold colour'. In 1830 Cook's *Typography of Wales* understandably warned that this 'should on no account be taken in the afternoons'. More pleasant refreshment can be had near the market at the Spinning Wheel, the Llanerch Inn and the Hampton.

Llandudno (Gwynedd)
Where: Market Street
When: Monday to Saturday, half-day Wednesday
What: fish, pottery, pet foods, greengrocery, sweets, hardware

The Llandudno market is a very small one, consisting of the six stalls named above. Negotiations are under way to build a shopping precinct on this site, and this would feature a new market. The Cottage Loaf in Market Street is recommended for lunch.

Llanfyllin (Powys)
Where: High Street
When: Thursday
What: fruit, vegetables, fish, bedding plants, conifers, new and nearly-new clothes, pet supplies, bric-à-brac, china, toys, occasionally cakes

The number of stalls in the Llanfyllin market varies according to the weather, but the mere fact that there is a market at all brings a lot of extra trade into the town on a Thursday from the surrounding Powys countryside. Llanfyllin was granted its charter in 1293 by Llywelyn ap Gruffydd ap Gwenwynwyn, Lord of Mechain. Along with Welshpool it is one of the only two Welsh boroughs to have received charters from native Welsh rulers.

In July every year the town holds a festival of music which attracts top professional musicians and draws audiences from a wide area. The town is also famous for its flowers, having won numerous awards for colourful parks and gardens.

A visitor to the market can choose from what must be one of the longest bar menus in the country at the 360-year-old Cain Valley Hotel, which is open all day on market day and has log fires in the winter. A beef omelette, black pudding, trout cooked in butter with chips and a 'farmer's breakfast' of chopped ham and onions in scrambled eggs are among the dishes on offer. Another speciality of the hotel is real ale.

Llangollen (Clwyd)
Where: Market Street car-park
When: Tuesday
What: fruit and vegetables, plants, household goods, carpets, clothes, sewing materials, bric-à-brac, pet foods

It is well worth visiting the Llangollen Weavers, where you can see fabrics being woven, and demonstrations of hand-weaving on 150-year-old looms can be arranged. Fabrics, clothes, rugs and wool are for sale in the mill shop. A prime time to visit Llangollen is during the Eisteddfod, usually held in July. Entries from more than thirty countries compete in singing and dancing contests. There are plenty of places to eat – in Bridge Street try Gales food and wine bar or Le Jardin; in Castle St Burnett's, Cegin Collen or Cottage Tea Rooms; in Market Street the Coffee Pot.

London
Some London markets have been established for centuries, but new ones are springing up all the time. This list is not exhaustive, but it does include most of the London markets which are of special interest to the visitor.

Bayswater Road
Where: Bayswater Road
When: Sunday morning
How: buses 12, 88; tube station Lancaster Gate (Central line)

Sells tourist souvenirs, mainly paintings, etchings and reproductions, also leather belts, tea-towels, Beefeater dolls.

Bermondsey
Where: Bermondsey Square, SE1
When: Friday
How: buses 1, 42, 78, 189; tube stations Borough (Northern line), Elephant and Castle (Bakerloo line)

Bermondsey market, or the New Caledonian as it is also known, is the main dealers' market for antiques in London and south-east England. Trading between dealers begins at about 3 a.m. or even earlier, and most of the serious business is over by breakfast-time, when the general public starts to arrive. The market's forerunner, the Old Caledonian, opened in 1855 on the Copenhagen fields in Islington. It had its heyday as a junk and antiques market in the '20s and '30s, when it was a well-loved feature of London life. Closed by the War in 1939, it opened ten years later on its present site. Hot drinks and hot dogs are available from a van in the market, traditional breakfasts from cafés nearby. The Hand and Marigold opens on Friday at 7.30 a.m.

Berwick Street
Where: Berwick Street and Rupert Street, Soho, W1
When: Monday to Saturday
How: buses 1, 7, 8, 14, 15, 19, 22, 25, 38, 55, 73, 88, 159; tube stations Oxford Circus (Victoria, Central and Bakerloo lines), Piccadilly Circus (Bakerloo and Piccadilly lines), Tottenham Court Road (Central and Northern lines)

Probably London's best fruit and vegetable market, specializing in the earliest and choicest produce from Britain and abroad, and in unusual and exotic fruit. Berwick Street has been a market for 200 years. It was the first to sell tomatoes (in 1880) and grapefruit (1890); it was also among the first to install electric light. Busiest time is lunch-time, when the market is full of office workers. Huge choice of restaurants nearby, particularly good for Chinese and Italian food.

Billingsgate
Where: new market, West India Dock, E14; old market, Lower Thames Street, EC3
When: new market, Tuesday to Saturday (5.30 a.m.–10 a.m.)
How: new market, buses 5, 15, 23, 40, 56, 106, 277, N84, N95; old market hall, Monument tube station (Circle and District lines)

Billingsgate has been a fish market since Saxon times and it was a sad day when it was moved in 1982 from its ancient riverside site to the new location at the Isle of Dogs. The splendid Victorian buildings with their façade of brick and stone and ornamental cast-iron, the cold, dark, wet, fish hall, the slippery cobbles, antiquated freezers and inadequate parking were as much a part of a fishmerchant's life as his bobbing hat, made of leather and cork for carrying fish boxes on his head. Today's Billingsgate is grey and characterless, but very efficient. Trading lasts from 5.30 a.m. until 10 a.m. and buying by telephone continues until lunch-time.

Brick Lane
Where: Brick Lane, Cheshire Street, Cygnet Street, Bacon Street, Chilton Street, E1
When: Sunday morning
How: buses 5, 8, 22, 35, 47, 149; tube station Liverpool Street (Central, Metropolitan and Circle lines; British Rail)

A sprawling and diverse market, Brick Lane is very cheap, but purchasers always run the risk of buying stolen or faulty goods, and traders do not hang around to wait for complaints. The best bargains are to be had at daybreak. The purchaser is legally entitled to goods bought in an open market in daylight hours. In Brick Lane itself are fruit, vegetables and canned food, and in the surrounding streets crockery, electrical equipment, records, furniture, tools, shoes, antiques and jewellery. Chilton Street has a popular bicycle market. Brick Lane market is a platform for people's opinions, political and otherwise, and there is often quite a strong police presence there, though rarely any trouble. Local Pakistanis have established some excellent and cheap curry houses in the area.

Brixton
Where: Electric Avenue, Atlantic Road, Brixton Station Road, Market Row, SW9
When: Monday to Saturday, half-day Wednesday
How: buses 2, 3, 35, 50, 95, 109, 159; tube station: Brixton (Victoria line)

London's best and liveliest daily market, Brixton has over 300 stalls, arcade kiosks and shops in and around the railway arches, selling an enormous variety of goods including food, second-hand clothes, records and cheap jewellery. It has the best selection of Caribbean food in London, with a dozen or so fishmongers selling shark and goat fish among other sorts. Yams, plantains, ugli fruit, kola nuts, cassava flour, pigs' ears and tails, and reggae records are other specialities.

Camden Lock

Where: Commercial Place, Camden High Street, Chalk Farm Road, NW1
When: Saturday and Sunday
How: buses 3, 24, 31, 53, 68, 74; tube station: Camden Town (Northern line)

Camden Lock began in 1973 when a handful of craftsmen set up workshops there. The market selling their knitwear, jewellery, pottery and leather opened the following year and has since become both fashionable and more expensive. Besides arts and crafts there are chinoiserie, second-hand clothes, Art Deco and antiques, wholefoods, herbs and musical instruments. Dingwall's dance hall and eating house, famous for rock and jazz, is in the heart of the Lock. The market has now expanded into the Old Stables and Primrose Market, beyond the Roundhouse.

Camden Passage

Where: Camden Passage, Islington, N1
When: Wednesday morning, Saturday
How: buses 4, 19, 30, 38, 43, 73, 171, 172, 277, 279; tube station: Angel (Northern line)

Camden Passage is a charming and prosperous antique market that was established in 1960. It is not cheap, but it does sell a vast selection of Art Deco, Art Nouveau, china, silver, clocks, antique toys, prints and maps. The outside stalls selling jewellery, china, and bric-à-brac are cheaper than the shops inside the Georgian

Village, but still not cheap. There are plenty of up-market places to eat, including Frederick's. Aquilino's has good Italian food at reasonable prices.

Club Row
Where: Sclater Street, E1
When: Sunday morning
How: buses 5, 8, 22, 35, 47, 149; tube station Liverpool Street (Central, Metropolitan and Circle lines; British Rail)

The open-air pet market at Club Row off Brick Lane began about 300 years ago as an illegal overspill from the livestock market – a way of avoiding market tolls. Conditions surrounding trading at Club Row have always been controversial: in the nineteenth century it sold songbirds in tiny cages; in the 1930s linnets and thrushes could be bought in paper bags. In 1934 an Act of Parliament outlawed the sale of British birds, but traders at Club Row continued to prosper. The market expanded to sell pets and poultry. Birds and animals were often painted to look like more exotic species – many were ill or had been maltreated or stolen. Today the RSPCA regularly inspects the licensed traders and campaigners against cruelty to animals patrol the street, but there are still a few unscrupulous dealers about.

Columbia Road
Where: Columbia Road, E2
When: Sunday morning
How: buses 6, 8, 35, 55; tube station Old Street (Northern line)

In 1869 Baroness Burdett-Coutts provided £200,000 for the building of the Columbia Market, a huge Gothic-cathedral-like edifice intended as a shelter for costermongers and their wares. But the costermongers did not like the market and refused to use it. The building was demolished in 1960. The market that does thrive in Columbia Road is the Sunday morning flower market, the only one of its kind in London. It sells bulbs, roses, bedding plants, shrubs, trees, house-plants, compost, pots, hanging baskets, and dried and artificial flowers, as well as cut flowers. Prices get cheaper as lunch-time approaches and some of the merchandise is auctioned off. As is the East End custom, the Birdcage serves free sea-food with lunchtime drinks.

Farringdon Road
Where: Farringdon Road, EC1
When: Monday to Saturday, weather permitting
How: buses 5, 55, 63, 168A, 221, 243, 259; tube station Farringdon (Circle line)

Books have been sold here since Dickens' day. It is a small market of about half a dozen stalls, all run by one man and specializing in second-hand books. They vary in price from a few pence to hundreds of pounds and the market is frequented by book dealers from all over London looking for bargains. The site itself is dirty, smelly and noisy with traffic. Graham Greene wrote: 'A sunk railway track and a gin distillery flank the gritty street. There is something Victorian about the whole place – an air of ugly commercial endeavour mixed with old idealisms and philanthropies.'

Greenwich
Where: Greenwich Church Street, Greenwich High Road, SE10
When: Saturday, Sunday
How: buses 1, 53, 177, 180, 188; British Rail; boat from Westminster or Charing Cross

A very lively market, in several locations, selling antiques, bric-à-brac, second-hand clothes, crafts, books and records.

Jubilee Market and Covent Garden Market
Where: Jubilee Hall and Covent Garden Piazza, WC2
When: every day, antiques on Monday
How: buses 1, 6, 9, 13, 55, 77, 170; tube station Covent Garden (Piccadilly line)

The Covent Garden Piazza was designed in 1631 by Inigo Jones on the site of a forty-acre garden that had belonged to the monks of Westminster Abbey before the Dissolution of the Monasteries. It quickly became the country's most important wholesale market for fruit, vegetables and flowers. The market continued expanding until 1974, when the Piazza became too small to hold it, and it was moved to its new site at Nine Elms. The original buildings were preserved and renovated, and opened again in 1980. Covent Garden, with its wine bars, chic restaurants and expensive specialist shops has become very fashionable and the market is a great tourist attraction. There are still bargains to be had in the antiques market, and the general market provides office workers with provisions and other basic items not available elsewhere in the area; but the crafts – jewellery, toys, pottery and knitwear – are on the whole expensive. Buskers, jugglers and mime artists entertain the crowds. The atmosphere is relaxed and self-conscious. (See also New Covent Garden.)

Kingsland Waste
Where: Kingsland Road, E8
When: Monday to Saturday
How: buses 22, 38, 48, 67, 149, 243; train: Dalston Junction (from Broad Street)

This market is situated in the slip road parallel to Kingsland Road and is well known for spare parts of all kinds, mechanical and electrical, in which it has traded for the past fifty years. It has everything for the do-it-yourself enthusiast from paints and tools to door locks. Other stalls sell records and imported clothes. There is a small selection of cheap tinned goods – shoppers can walk the short distance to Ridley Road (see page 115) for a wide variety of fresh food.

Leadenhall
Where: Gracechurch Street, EC3
When: Monday to Friday
How: buses 10, 15, 25, 35, 40, 48; tube stations Bank (Central and Northern lines), Monument (District and Circle lines)

Leadenhall gets its name from a lead-roofed mansion built there in the fourteenth century for Sir Hugh Neville. When it was destroyed by fire, the City authorities established a poultry market, where poultry-sellers who were not freemen of the city were obliged to trade. In 1881 Sir Horace Jones, architect of Smithfield and Billingsgate, designed the present spacious and imposing building with its stone arches and glass roof. Since that time the market has specialized in all kinds of high-quality fresh provisions. It is the place to go for quail and guinea fowl, hare and venison as well as the Christmas turkey; the fish stalls sell oysters and lobster. An interesting place for a lunch-time stroll, with refreshment at the Lamb, New Moon and Bunch of Grapes, as well as a number of snack bars.

Leather Lane

Where: Leather Lane, EC1
When: Monday to Saturday
How: buses 5, 8, 18, 19, 22, 25, 38, 45, 55, 171; tube stations Chancery Lane (Central line), Farringdon (Circle and Metropolitan lines)

This market's busiest time is lunch-time, when it is full of office workers from Holborn and the Gray's Inn Road. It sells a wide variety of goods – cheap, good quality fruit and vegetables, flowers and plants, hardware, clothes, handbags and toiletries. It has never been a leather market – the name derives from the Flemish Le Vrun Lane, which it was called in medieval times. By 1598 it was known as Lither Lane and was 'narrow and dirty, lined with stalls and barrows and itinerant dealers in fish, bacon, vegetables and old clothes', according to a contemporary account. Today it is one of London's most prosperous street markets.

New Covent Garden

Where: between Nine Elms Lane and Wandsworth Road, SW8
When: Monday to Friday; Saturdays in summer
How: buses 44, 170, N88, 77, N68

The sixty-acre site at Nine Elms Lane was opened in 1974 and replaced the old Covent Garden as Britain's foremost wholesale fruit and vegetable market, handling produce from about seventy countries, as well as that grown at home. It is not a picturesque place like the old market, but it is extremely efficient and easily accessible to large lorries. Trading takes place in two long parallel buildings connected by walkways where there are banks, pubs and cafés. Traders pay for the space they rent – display space inside the buildings and a service area behind it. Vehicles pay on entry. Flowers are sold in a vast polyester and glass 'greenhouse' where the temperature is controlled and the air filtered.

Petticoat Lane

Where: Middlesex Street, Goulston Street, Wentworth Street, Bell Lane, Cobb Street, Leyden Street and Toynbee Street, Aldgate, E1
When: the whole market opens on Sunday mornings; parts of it also open Monday to Friday, 10.30 a.m.–2.30 p.m.
How: buses 5, 10, 11, 15, 22, 23, 25, 40, 67, 78, 149; tube stations: Aldgate (Metropolitan and Circle lines), Aldgate East (Metropolitan and District lines), Liverpool Street (Central, Metropolitan and Circle lines)

Petticoat Lane was rechristened Middlesex Street by the Victorians, but the market remains famous for its clothes, which have been sold here since the eighteenth century. The Lane was originally outside the city wall, and after 1290 it became a refuge for the Jews who defied banishment from the country; it was they who first started the trade in second-hand clothes. Today most of the clothes are new and pretty much as offered on any other street market, except for the wide range of leather garments. The prices are not cheap. There are also antique and modern jewellery and watches. Many of the goods have 'fallen off the backs of lorries'.

Portobello Road

Where: Portobello Road, Golbourne Road, Notting Hill, W11
When: Monday to Saturday, half-day Thursday

How: buses 7, 15, 23, 27, 28, 31, 52; tube stations Notting Hill Gate (Central, District and Circle lines), Ladbroke Grove (Metropolitan line), Westbourne Park (Metropolitan line)

Portobello Road was originally a lane leading to a farm of that name. The area was built up in the 1860s and a market started here about twenty years later. It began with the basics of fruit and vegetables, and expanded in the 1950s to include antiques, for which it is particularly famous today. The market is liveliest on Saturdays, when it extends for almost a mile. From Chepstow Villas to Lonsdale Road are expensive specialist stalls for collectors. Further down is a mixture of bric-à-brac and ethnic food, especially Caribbean. North of Tavistock Road are stalls with lots of household junk. Under the flyover is a bicycle market, with viewing at noon and an auction at 2 p.m.

Ridley Road
Where: Ridley Road, Dalston E8
When: Monday to Saturday
How: buses 22, 30, 38, 48, 67, 76, 149, 243, 277; train: Dalston Junction (BR North London Line)

There has been a market here since the 1850s, but trading really began to boom in the 1930s. At that time Oswald Mosley used the market for his Fascist platform and there were violent clashes between rival political groups. Today Ridley Road is a very lively market with a Caribbean flavour, at its best on Fridays and Saturdays. It offers a huge selection of food – European, Jewish and West Indian, as well as reggae music, bright fabrics and clothes, handbags and household goods. The Kingsland High Road nearby has branches of all the major shops and a very attractive pie and mash house.

Shepherd's Bush
Where: along the railway viaduct between Shepherd's Bush and Goldhawk Road stations, Shepherd's Bush, W12

When: Monday to Saturday, half-day Thursday
How: buses 12, 72, 105, 207, 220, 237; tube stations Shepherd's
Bush (Metropolitan and Central lines), Goldhawk Road
(Metropolitan line)

The railway was built in 1864 and the market started in 1919 on land
leased from the railway. Today's tenants pay their rent to London
Transport. Shepherd's Bush is a cosmopolitan market with lock-up
shops under the railway viaduct arches as well as mobile stalls. It
caters for Indian, West Indian and Arab customers and offers a
wide variety of ethnic food – meat and fish as well as fruit and
vegetables – carpets, curtains, luxury goods, underwear and toys,
especially at Christmas time. It is also a good place to look for gas
cookers (new and second-hand) and electrical goods.

Smithfield
Where: between West Smithfield and Charterhouse Street, EC1
When: Monday to Friday, 5 a.m.–9 a.m.
How: buses 4, 8, 22, 25, 63, 221; tube stations Farringdon or
Barbican (Circle and Metropolitan lines), Chancery Lane (Central
line)

The oldest and largest wholesale meat market in Europe – the last
of London's great medieval markets still on its original site.

Long Eaton (Derbyshire)
Where: Market Place, off Tamworth Road
When: Wednesday, Friday, Saturday, and see below
What: fruit, vegetables, provisions, meat, fabrics, clothing,
household, second-hand goods, bric-à-brac

The village of Sawley, now joined with Long Eaton, was granted a
charter to hold markets and a Michaelmas Fair in 1258. Today there
is a Wakes Fair in August and a carnival in late June. There is a flea
market in the Market Place every Tuesday, and a number of pubs in
the vicinity serve real ale.

Loughborough (Leicestershire)
Where: Market Place, Cattle Market and Ward's End
When: Thursday, Saturday
What: clothes, shoes, plants, fruit, vegetables, hardware, linen, hosiery, fish, meat, fabrics

Loughborough's market was granted by charter in 1206, as was the annual fair, which still takes place today in November through the streets of the town centre. Snacks and light meals can be had at the Town Hall, and the Lord Nelson, the Barley Mow and the Griffin are three pubs within easy reach of the market.

Lowestoft (Suffolk)
Where: Triangle, Old Market Street
When: Friday, Saturday
What: fruit, vegetables, flowers, fish, provisions, clothes, and seaside gear in the summer

Fishing was Lowestoft's main industry from the middle of the last century until recently and it is still an excellent place to shop for all kinds of freshly caught and smoked fish. An eighteenth-century smoke-house is still in use in Raglan Street. A Sunday market is held on Lowestoft North Denes below the lighthouse, which is also the site of the Spring Fair, offering rides and other entertainments as well as produce and confectionery. As a seaside town, Lowestoft has a wide selection of eating places, cafés, pubs and restaurants specializing in sea-food. The Martello Café in Sparrow's Nest Park caters for visitors to the Sunday market.

Ludlow (Shropshire)
Where: Town Hall and Castle Square
When: Monday, Friday, Saturday
What: basically a food market, but it does have fabrics and antiques too

There is a May Fair on the first weekend in May. The Angel Hotel and De Grey's Restaurant are both in Broad Street, and there are ten other places to eat within five minutes' walk of the market.

Luton (Bedfordshire)
Where: The Arndale Centre, Church Street
When: Monday to Saturday (half-day Wednesday)
What: meat, fish, fruit, vegetables, clothes, textiles, garden plants, bulbs, biscuits, bags, toys, house-plants, flowers, china, newspapers, snacks, carpets, suitcases, eggs

Luton market has been in existence for almost a thousand years and was mentioned in the Domesday Book. In 1612 the Manor of Luton, which included the market, passed to Sir Robert Napier, owner of Luton Hoo. Eight years later a grant was made to the Napier family for two fairs or marts to be held in Luton, on the Feast of St Mark (25 April) and the Feast of St Luke (18 October). In 1795 there was an acute food shortage and an angry crowd attacked dealers who were trying to buy up the available corn on market day. Soldiers were called in to suppress the riot. Another thing that angered the public was that the market was still in private ownership. In 1850 Mr J. S. Leigh, the current Lord of the Manor, agreed to lease the market to the newly established Board of Health for seventy-five years at £150 per year, provided that the town built a new corn exchange and market house costing no less than £2,000. The foundations were laid in 1868 and a temporary wooden building was erected, only to be burned down on Bonfire Night the same year. The new Corn Exchange was finally opened in 1869 and at the same time the Board of Health built the Plait Halls in Cheapside to house the market for straw plait.

In 1911 Parliament gave Luton corporation the opportunity to buy the ancient rights of markets and fairs from the Lord of the Manor, who at that time was Sir Julius Wernher. The Plait Halls kept going until 1925, when they were put out of business by foreign trade, and twenty-five years later the Corn Exchange also closed because of lack of business. The covered market at Cheapside continued to serve Luton, but as the town boomed with the growth of its motor industry and its airport, it became necessary to move to larger, more hygienic and comfortable premises. The development of the Arndale Centre was the result: it was opened in 1972 and hailed as an outstanding triumph of modern planning, with its 145 stalls, multi-storey car-park, fluorescent lighting and gas-fired central heating and air-conditioning. An efficient refuse system, lifts, meat-and-vegetable-preparation rooms, ample unloading and storage space, and a restroom for the traders were other improvements on the old hall at Cheapside.

Lymington (Hampshire)
Where: High Street
When: Saturday
What: a general range of goods

Macclesfield (Cheshire)
Where: at the side of the Town Hall (outdoor market); at Waters Green; at the Grosvenor Centre (indoor market)
When: Town Hall market on Tuesday, Friday and Saturday; Waters Green on Saturday; Grosvenor Centre, Tuesday to Saturday
What: fresh and tinned goods, health foods, pet foods, clothes, fabrics, household, cheese

Macclesfield has a Wakes Fair in October. You can eat at the Bull's Head, Market Place; at Bate Hall, Chestergate; or at Brambles, Jordangate. All are within five minutes' walk of the market.

Maidenhead (Berkshire)
Where: King Street
When: Tuesday, Friday, Saturday
What: fruit, vegetables, plants, hardware, fabrics, clothes

Lunch is served at the Brewer's Tea House in King Street and at the Bear Hotel, High Street.

Maidstone (Kent)
Where: Lockmeadow, Barker Road
When: Tuesday
What: fruit, vegetables, meat, fish, clothing, antiques, bric-à-brac, household, records, stationery, jewellery, flowers, plants, soft furnishings, pet foods, crockery

Maidstone has a large livestock market on Mondays and in addition there are thirty-one sheep and cattle fairs each year. On general market days and Fridays there is an auction of farm produce in the Agricultural Hall. The Hall is also the venue for antiques and furniture sales, exhibitions, dog shows, wrestling, five-a-side football, archery competitions and bull shows. Maidstone market charter dates from 1549, but records show that Archbishop Boniface obtained a grant from Henry III in 1261 to hold a weekly market in the town. The 1549 charter was occasionally withdrawn because of misconduct by the citizens of Maidstone. The original market was held in the town centre, but it spilled over into the surrounding streets and had to be moved in 1824 to its present position because of danger from the London to Dover traffic. The market has two mobile catering vans, six ice-cream vans and two fish-and-chip vans. Its large antiques and bric-à-brac section attracts dealers who come early to buy before the general public arrives. Maidstone has an annual carnival and a River Festival, usually in July.

Maldon (Essex)
Where: behind the White Horse in the town centre
When: Thursday, Saturday
What: produce, hardware, fabrics

The Oakwood Arts Centre holds exhibitions and craft markets and has a coffee bar specializing in waffles and cream teas. There is a carnival on the first Saturday in August.

Malton (North Yorkshire)
Where: Market Place
When: Saturday
What: fruit, vegetables, wet fish, cakes, biscuits, sweets, clothes, bedding, leather goods, plants, bicycles, car accessories, electrical goods

On Tuesday and Friday there are fatstock markets held in the centre of Malton, which is a small market town of Roman origin. The museum in the Market Square provides a detailed history of the town. There are several pubs in and around the Market Place offering a good selection of beers and wines, and many also serve bar meals. There is also a café and a restaurant. An annual fair is held in mid-November on Wentworth Street car-park. In addition the Malton Show in July promotes local arts, crafts and sports.

Malvern (Hereford and Worcester)
Where: Car-park, Edith Walk
When: Friday
What: general goods, fruit, vegetables, etc

Malvern celebrates the Malvern Festival, the Three Counties show and Victorian Week. Near the market are the Beauchamp Hotel, the Unicorn Inn, the Red Lion, the Foley Arms Hotel and Mount Pleasant Hotel. What you should drink with lunch is Malvern water, which has been renowned since the Middle Ages for its purity and freshness: references to St Ann's Well date from 1282. In 1558 Queen Elizabeth I brought the Holy Well into English history by granting the spring to the Lord of the Manor, John Hornyold, under the Great Seal. The Eye Well's reputation for curing sore eyes was confirmed in 1622 in Bannister's Breviary of the Eye:

> *A little more of their curing tell*
> *How they helped sore eyes with a new found well*
> *Great speech of the Malvern Hills was late recorded*
> *Unto which spring people in troops resorted.*

Malvern was established as a leading spa by the Victorian era and
today its water enjoys new popularity as the Queen's favourite
drink.

Manchester
Manchester city centre has two markets – one in Church Street,
which opens daily with a few stalls specializing in gramophone
records, tapes and second-hand books; and one in the Arndale
Centre, High Street, which is also open daily and is a large covered
market with about 180 stalls. There are numerous other markets
just a bus ride away from Manchester City centre:

Altrincham, Market Hall and open market. Tuesday and Saturday
are full market days with over 230 stalls; Friday is produce only with
40 stalls offering the best in cheeses, cooked meats, fruit and
vegetables.
Ashton-in-Makerfield, outdoor market on Tuesday and Saturday.
Ashton-under-Lyme, Market Hall and open market, both open
daily except Tuesday. Particularly noted for textiles, fruit and
vegetables.
Atherton, outdoor market every Friday.
Beswick, open market held in Grey Mare Lane every Monday,
Wednesday, Friday and Saturday.
Bolton, Market Hall and open market. The Market Hall is open
daily except Wednesday afternoon and has 200 stalls including a fish
market. The large open market is held Tuesday, Thursday and
Saturday.
Bury, (see page 42)
Denton, a small general market held Wednesday, Friday and
Saturday.
Droylsden, a small market of 35 stalls held on Tuesday and
Saturday.
Eccles, open market on Tuesday, Thursday and Saturday.
Farnworth, large general market on Mondays, Fridays and
Saturdays.
Glossop (see page 69).

Gorton, open market on Tuesday, Friday and Saturday; indoor food hall open daily except Wednesday.

Harpurhey, open market Tuesday, Friday and Saturday; food hall open daily.

Heywood, Market Hall open Friday and Saturday specializing in dairy produce.

Hindley, open market every Friday.

Hollinwood, small open market held in Hollins Road every Thursday.

Horwich, open market on Tuesday and Friday.

Hyde, Market Hall and open market. Market Hall open daily except Monday; large outdoor market on Wednesday, Thursday, Friday and Saturday, particularly noted for textiles and clothes.

Leigh, outdoor and indoor markets held Wednesday, Thursday, Friday and Saturday.

Longsight, outdoor market on Wednesday, Friday and Saturday.

Middleton, open market and food hall on Friday and Saturday.

Mossley, small general market on Thursday.

Moss Side, Market Hall in shopping precinct complex open daily except Wednesday.

New Mills, small outdoor market on Friday and Saturday.

Newton Heath, open market on Monday, Wednesday and Saturday.

Oldham (see page 138).

Partington, open market on Tuesday and Saturday.

Pendlebury, large open market held Tuesday, Friday and Saturday.

Radcliffe, indoor market open on Tuesday, Friday and Saturday.

Ramsbottom, small open market held every Saturday.

Rochdale (see page 149).

Royton, open market every Thursday.

Salford, large open market and food hall. Market held Monday, Wednesday, Friday and Saturday; food hall open daily except Tuesday.

Shaw-Crompton Market, Westway, open market held every Thursday.

Stalybridge, Market Hall and small open market open daily except Tuesday.

Stockport (see page 167).

Swinton, small open market held Tuesday, Thursday and Saturday.
Tyldesley, open market on Friday.
Urmston, open market on Tuesday, Friday and Saturday.
Walkden, Market Hall open all week except Wednesday.
Westhoughton, covered market on Thursday and Saturday.
Whitefield, small open market on Thursday.
Wigan, indoor and outdoor markets held daily.
Wilmslow, open market on Friday.
Wythenshawe, open market on Tuesday, Friday and Saturday;
indoor food hall open daily.

Market Harborough (Leicestershire)
Where: Northampton Road, adjoining the cattle market
When: Tuesday
What: general retail goods and produce

Market Harborough was created by Henry II as a market centre –
the first mention of the market is in 1204. The market has been held
on a Tuesday ever since 1221. Up to 1903 the main square was the
venue for this weekly event, but in that year the present cattle
market premises were opened in Springfield Street, where cattle,
sheep, calves, pigs and poultry are bought and sold every week. The
general produce market was transferred from the square to covered
accommodation adjoining the cattle market in 1938.

Marlborough (Wiltshire)
Where: High Street
When: Monday to Saturday, half-day Wednesday
What: greengrocery, clothing, flowers, hardware, wool, health
foods, fresh fish, cheeses, bric-à-brac

As a stopping point on the stagecoach route from London to Bath,
Marlborough became the commercial centre for a large area of
Wiltshire. The Georgian High Street has numerous good pubs – one
is the Sun. There is an annual Mop Fair in October.

Maryport (Cumbria)
Where: Lower Church Street
When: Friday (outdoor), Thursday and Friday (indoor)
What: a general market with fruit and vegetables; clothes and knitting wool a speciality. A very good selection of fish in the indoor market

The market was originally held in Fleming Square and sold mainly local produce. Although the butter market building itself has gone, the cobbled square remains. The market is now held in Lower Church Street, with the back doors of the indoor market, in Senhouse Street, opposite. There are various cafés nearby and the Golden Lion Hotel and Waverley Hotel offer bar meals. The annual carnival week is held in the first week of July and culminates in a grand parade on the Saturday.

Matlock (Derbyshire)
Where: next to bus station in Imperial Road
When: Tuesday, Friday
What: fruit, vegetables, meat, wool, leather goods, men's wear, towels, sweets, children's clothes, cheese

There are many places to eat within walking distance of the market. Matlock has a carnival in August and, like the rest of the Derbyshire Dale towns, is noted for its custom of well-dressing, a ceremony of thanksgiving for water, which originated in pre-Christian days when the life-giving springs were worshipped as gods. Today the custom is a Christian ceremony – thousands of flower petals are collected and pressed into a clay tablet in the form of a picture representing a Biblical scene; it is then erected over the well and blessed by clergymen of all denominations.

Melton Mowbray (Leicestershire)
Where: Market Place
When: Tuesday, Saturday

What: greengrocery, clothing, crafts and gifts. Melton Mowbray pork pies are a speciality, as is local Stilton cheese. A cattle market is held on Tuesday

Melton market has over a thousand years of trading behind it. It was chartered before 1077 and is the only one in Leicestershire to appear in the Domesday Book. Take a look at the Swan Porch on the south side of the Market Place – the building was the house of a wool merchant in the Middle Ages, and later a coaching inn. On the north side there is Ye Olde Pork Pie Shoppe. Pork pies were first made here in the early years of the last century and are now famous the world over. They caught on quickly in Melton because, along with a hunk of Stilton cheese made with milk from the surrounding rich pasturelands, they were a good snack to put in the saddlebags of the hunt. The fox has been hunted by Meltonians for over 200 years and the territories of the Belvoir, Quorn and Cottesmore Hunts all adjoin the Market Place, where the hunts meet on New Year's Day.

In the Market Place are the Cosmopolitan, the Fish Shop and the Baker's Oven. Melton Day is held on the May Bank Holiday.

Milton Keynes (Buckinghamshire)
Where: shopping centre
When: Tuesday, Saturday; Thursday, antiques and bric-à-brac
What: 'Everything from cabbages and socks to radios'

There are places to eat within the shopping centre. Milton Keynes has a fireworks show and funfair in aid of charity in November.

Mold (Clwyd)
Where: High Street, Daniel Owen Street
When: Wednesday, Saturday
What: a wide selection of goods including leisure clothing, ladies' fashions, home-brewing and wine-making equipment, toys, second-hand books, prints, bread, cheese, bacon, fruit, vegetables, basketware, pet foods, motor accessories, electrical accessories, jewellery, crafts

The Mold markets have been operating since 1835. A record of a grant to the Lord of the Manor of Mold (or Mould, as it was) marked '6th George II 14th December' is to be found on the patent rolls between 1700 and 1846. In addition to the street markets, Mold Traders Hall houses 17 permanent market stalls and has been open since 1976. Excellent catering premises provide snacks, bar meals or more substantial fare. The home of the Welsh playwright, Daniel Owen, now forms part of Y Pentan public house, situated adjacent to the market areas.

Monmouth (Gwent)
Where: underneath the arches of the Shirehall and on the cobbles of the forecourt
When: Friday (about 20 traders) and Saturday (about 10 traders)
What: greengroceries, antique jewellery, second-hand books, fish, and garden requisites

Monmouth general market has been in existence in various forms since the eleventh century and in sites in various parts of the town. In the 1930s it was housed in the new market building in Priory Street, where it remained until the building was gutted by fire in 1967. The market was then moved to Agincourt Square – its original site of 900 years earlier. The type of goods sold has changed little since the 1800s, except that clothing and furnishing fabrics have replaced live poultry. It is a typical country market, crowded and very busy, especially on Fridays. The King's Head Hotel, the Beaufort Hotel, the Punch House and the Bull Inn offer refreshments at lunch-time, and there are pleasure fairs in May and August.

Montgomery (Powys)
Where: town centre
When: Thursday
What: home-made cakes, fresh fish, bric-à-brac, fruit and vegetables

Montgomery has a May Fair on the first Thursday in May. The Checkers Hotel and the Castle Kitchen Tea Shop can be recommended for lunch (the latter serves wholefoods).

Motherwell (Strathclyde)
There are two markets in Motherwell:

Where: Bellshill market, Hamilton Road
When: Monday
What: food, clothing and household goods

Bellshill market is particularly noted for its huge range of quality net curtains. The Flamingo Snooker Club in Main Street and the Hattonrigg Hotel in Hattonrigg Road have a friendly atmosphere and cater for families.

Where: Wisham market, Caledonian Road
When: Saturday
What: food, fruit, vegetables, clothing

The Hub in Stewarton Street serves good food and caters for children.

Nantwich (Cheshire)
Where: Market Hall and adjacent open-air market, Churchyard Side
When: Thursday morning
What: general provisions, fruit, vegetables, household goods, curtaining, antiques, and see below

Nantwich is an ancient market town dating back to Roman times. The town centre has many fine half-timbered sixteenth-century buildings and is a paradise for antique collectors. As well as antique shops there are antiques markets on the first Thursday of each month except May, and on most Bank Holidays from 11 a.m. to 9 p.m. in the Civic Hall, Churchyard Side. The Red Cow in Beam Street near the market provides a good pub lunch. In Hospital Street is Churche's Mansion, a half-timbered Tudor building with a good restaurant on the ground floor.

Neath (West Glamorgan)
Where: Green Street
When: daily
What: miscellaneous retail goods, specializing in traditional Welsh foods – faggots and peas, cockles, and laverbread

Newark-on-Trent (Nottinghamshire)
Where: Market Place, outdoors; indoor Butter Market on ground floor of the Town Hall, Market Place
When: outdoor market, Wednesday, Friday and Saturday; antiques and flea market on Monday. Butter Market has some stalls open throughout the week, but all are open on Wednesday, Friday and Saturday
What: about 170 stalls in the outdoor market sell fruit and vegetables, poultry, fish, cheese, flowers, plants, bulbs, seeds, clothes, basketwork, material, haberdashery, carpets, tools, jewellery, toiletries, second-hand books, cakes, biscuits, toys, linen, curtains, lace, crockery and double-glazing. The Butter Market has 38 stalls selling blinds, meat, poultry, flowers, bread, cakes, biscuits, Country and Western attire, pet food, crockery, kitchenware, lace, antiques, second-hand books, clothes, jewellery, key-cutting

There are various eating places and pubs around the Market Square. The King Charles I Coffee House is remarkable for its historic background – it is thought that Queen Henrietta Maria stayed here on her visit to the town during the Civil War. Meals, sandwiches and cakes are offered throughout the day at reasonable prices and the building itself is very attractive, being of half-timbered construction.

The Newark and Nottinghamshire Agricultural Show takes place at the Showground, Winthorpe, a few miles outside Newark every May and is a major event in the local calendar.

Newbury (Berkshire)
Where: Market Square
When: Thursday, Saturday
What: general, including local produce sale Thursday noon–4 p.m.

The Newbury Agricultural Show is held annually for one weekend around the middle of September. It features cattle, horses, sheep, pigs, farming equipment, show-jumping, leather goods, car sales and produce stalls. The Corn Exchange holds periodic antiques and collectors' fairs, as well as gardening exhibitions and cage-bird shows. The Waggon and Horses and the Hatchet, both near the market, are recommended for their good food.

Newcastle-under-Lyme (Staffordshire)
Where: 'The Stones', High Street (open market)
When: Monday, Tuesday (antiques market), Friday, Saturday
What: vegetables, fruit, fresh provisions, clothes, textiles, shoes, household goods (87 stalls)

Newcastle-under-Lyme's market was probably established near the new castle in the twelfth century. It soon moved to higher ground in High Street, where it has remained for over 700 years. High Street and Iron Market, which runs off it, were intended from the beginning to accommodate stalls and pens for livestock – hence their unusual width. High Street used to be at its widest near the church, and some stalls became permanent there, but most of the street, still known today as 'The Stones' after the cobbles that used to pave it, has been kept free for moveable stalls.

Newcastle market retains its traditional link with the Wakes. As Monday is the main market day, May Bank Holiday Monday has been chosen to celebrate the Newcastle Carnival, a tradition revived in 1973 to commemorate the 800th anniversary of the borough's first market charter. In conjunction with the council, the traders have brought back other outdoor entertainments, such as choirs and bands at Christmas and folk-dancing on other bank holidays. On May Day there is a special plant market for charity. Newcastle's cattle market, Smithfield, has been held off Blackfriars Road since 1871.

The Globe Café, the Old Coach House Restaurant and the Wine Vaults are all in the High Street.

Newcastle upon Tyne
Newcastle has four markets, ranging from the Bigg Market which dates back to Norman times, to the Greenmarket which was established just ten years ago:

Grainger Market and Arcade
Where: Grainger Street
When: Monday to Saturday, Wednesday half-day
What: about 250 stalls sell a wide range of convenience and durable goods. On Saturday tables are erected in the alleyways between stalls to offer poultry, eggs and plants

This market was opened in 1835 and several stalls have been occupied by the same tenants for many years – Marks and Spencer, for example, have had the same stall here for eighty years. When vacancies do arise there is always a queue of potential new traders. The General Weigh House is in alley no. 2, and this is an attraction with shoppers and visitors to the city.

Greenmarket
Where: Eldon Square
When: Monday to Saturday; late trading on Thursday until 7.30 p.m.
What: the essence of this market is its variety, which is ensured by the council when selecting tenants. It includes a fish and a plant market

The market was opened in 1976 as part of the Eldon Square development, which incorporates a shopping precinct and recreation centre. It is well served by local transport and there is ample parking. The market is enclosed, with air conditioning and a sophisticated security and fire-alarm system.

Quayside Sunday Market
Where: Quayside car-park
When: Sunday 10 a.m.–2.30 p.m.
What: A large variety of goods on as many as 200 stalls in summer

Before 1950 this market had more the character of a fair, for in addition to stalls selling confectionery, ice-cream, soft drinks, patent medicines, second-hand books, novelties and toys, there were traditional attractions such as strongmen, racing tipsters and games of skill and chance. Now the market has a more commercial character, but it still attracts up to 100,000 visitors a week. There are plans to develop craft trades in an enterprise village at the east end of the market.

Bigg Market
Where: near the Town Hall
When: Tuesday, Thursday, Saturday
What: 33 stalls selling traditional market goods

Newcastle's oldest market: the name 'Bigg' comes from a kind of barley no longer grown locally.

Newmarket (Suffolk)
Where: The Rookery, Market Square
When: Tuesday, Saturday
What: fresh produce, meat, fish, eggs, clothes, shoes

Newmarket is said to have risen to prominence in the thirteenth century when an outbreak of the plague forced the market of the village of Exning to move to a new site. By the time of the Tudors it was an important market town. Newmarket's connections with royalty and racing date from 1605 when James I stopped off at Newmarket and liked it so much that he built himself a hunting lodge there. Charles I and Charles II continued the royal trend. Sales of horses have been held in Newmarket since the 1870s; today they take place at Tattersalls Sales Paddocks off the Avenue, and there is free admittance to the public. The Bushell Inn is recommended for lunch. It claims to be the oldest in Newmarket, dating from the seventeenth century, and has a pit in the cellar where cock fights are supposed to have taken place. Many of the older buildings in the town were destroyed by the great fire of 1683, though a house in Palace Street that survived the fire is still standing today – it is said to have belonged to Charles II's mistress Nell Gwynne.

Newport (Gwent)
Where: between High Street and Upper Dock Street
When: Monday to Saturday
What: excellent fresh food, delicatessen, bakery, dairy produce, herbs, wholefoods, bric-à-brac, handicrafts, records, flowers, animal foods, bedding, curtains, medals

Newport was a market town in the Middle Ages, receiving its first charter in 1385. In 1847 a historian recorded that the Market House was used as a place for punishment as well as a 'mart for general goods' – here stood the whipping post and the stocks. The building was demolished as unsafe in 1793, an added nuisance being the invasion of cows from the cattle market next door. It was re-erected in 1864 and foundry marks from that date can still be seen in some of the girders of today's market. The market was expanded and given a vaulted roof in 1899, and a second storey in the 1930s provided the galleries which house four caterers and offer stall space to casual traders and smallholders on Fridays and Saturdays. The market facilities have recently been modernized, making it more hygienic, warmer and brighter without spoiling its Victorian character.

Good places to eat nearby are Murrenger House, a pub in High
Street; Simpson's Bar, High Street, sells real ale at low prices; and
Burlington Diner, Upper Dock Street, is an excellent cheap
transport café.

Newton Abbot (Devon)
Where: town centre
When: Monday to Saturday (covered market); Wednesday,
Saturday also open-air
What: the covered market sells fresh produce and provisions, and
the open-air market has a wide variety of general goods

Newton Abbot has a Cheese and Onion Fair in early September.
The Jolly Farmer is the pub nearest the market.

Newtown (Powys)
Where: covered market in Market Hall, Market Street; street
market in Broad Street and High Street
When: covered market Tuesday, Friday, Saturday; street market
Tuesday, Saturday
What: fruit, vegetables, fish, meat, household goods, clothes,
sweets, cheese

Newtown was granted a charter to hold markets by Edward I in
1277 and is still a flourishing market town, with a cattle market on
the last Tuesday in the month and on alternate Thursdays, and four
seasonal horse and pony fairs off Pool Road. There are several pubs
around the market that serve lunch.

Northallerton (North Yorkshire)
Where: High Street and Market Place
When: Wednesday, Saturday
What: fruit, vegetables, clothing, footwear, leather goods,

jewellery, materials, cheese, home-made produce, fish, tools, flowers, shrubs, potted plants, knitwear, double-glazing, bacon, floor coverings, cards, stationery, 50p stalls, books, electrical spares, sweets, pet food

Northallerton was a staging post for coaches travelling from London to the North, so it has always been a meeting centre. The market attracts large numbers of people from all over the North Riding. Recommended for refreshment are Betty's Tea Rooms, the Golden Lion and the Golden Fleece. The May Fair is held in the High Street on Bank Holiday Weekend and features swings, roundabouts and other rides.

Northampton
Where: Market Square and Sheep Street (for fish)
When: Wednesday, Friday, Saturday
What: fruit, cheese, clothes, sweets, vegetables, carpets, fresh and packaged goods, shoes (200 stalls)

On Tuesday there is an antiques market. Northampton Town Show is held annually on the last weekend in July. You can eat at Huckleberry's in Market Square or near the fishmarket at Kin Wa Chinese Restaurant in Sheep Street.

Northwich (Cheshire)
Where: Apple Market Street
When: Tuesday, Friday, Saturday
What: a general market

Northwich has a charter market dating back over five hundred years. A new market hall was opened in 1966, with a café and space for fifty-five traders (though in practice vendors often use more than one area). There are over 100 stalls outdoors, under a canopy.

Norwich (Norfolk)
Where: Market Place
When: Monday to Saturday
What: fruit, vegetables, excellent fish, meat, flowers, plants, tools,
coffee, tea, herbs, spices, jewellery, books, cards, bags, belts,
pictures, wools, textiles, fancy goods, health foods, seeds,
homeopathic remedies, cheese, snacks (including mushy peas,
chips, soup)

Norwich began as a market town more than a thousand years ago.
The Saxon market was in Tombland ('toom' meant 'empty land' –
nothing to do with tombs). Then the Norman conquerors built a
castle and established a new market, today's Provision Market,
close by. In 1096 the Norman bishop built the cathedral which
encroached on the Tombland market place, and this brought about
a fierce conflict between the townspeople and the monks of the
cathedral priory over market rights, which over a period of 350
years erupted in rioting and arson. The Norwich Easter Pleasure
Fair is still called the Tombland Fair, though Tombland has had
nothing to do with fairs or markets for hundreds of years. Until the
1930s the livestock market, the biggest in the country, was held at
Norwich Hill, which necessitated hundreds of sheep and cattle
being driven through the town centre every Saturday. Though this
was very picturesque, it was also unhygienic, unbusinesslike and
unkind; now there is a thirty-four-acre site at Harford where cattle
and thousands of pigs are cleanly, humanely and efficiently
marketed under cover, while the lorries are washed down and
disinfected. The Provision Market with its coloured awnings
remains one of the most delightful markets in the country. The
market pub is the Ironmongers Arms in St John Maddermarket.

Nottingham
Where: Victoria Centre, Glasshouse Street
When: daily
What: vast selection of cheap clothing, photographic goods, wigs,
electrical goods, footwear, fabrics, Nottingham lace, fish, meat,
poultry, fruit, vegetables, second-hand books

The history of Nottingham market goes back at least to Saxon times. The Normans created a new settlement round their castle with its own market, and the two existed side by side until about fifty years after the Conquest, when a new market was established on neutral ground. This became the focal point of the town – the Great Market Place and 'the fairest without exception of all England', as Leland described it in the sixteenth century. The pillory and tumbrel stood in the Market Place to punish 'forestallers' – people who bought from the growers on the way to town so that they could corner the market. Trading continued in the canvas-covered stalls of the Great Market Place until 1928, when the Central Market was opened. In 1972 the market was transferred again to its present site at the Victoria Centre, which also houses a shopping precinct. The Victoria Market has its own snack bars and licensed restaurant, offering fresh food at modest prices.

Nottingham's Sneiton Market is an open-air market in Bath Street selling clothing, footwear, materials, crockery, lino, carpets, watches, jewellery, toys, bulbs, plants, food, second-hand clothes, furniture, books, antique silver, bric-à-brac and stamps.

The Nottingham Goose Fair is held on Forest Recreation Ground on the first Thursday, Friday and Saturday in October. It was first mentioned in borough records in 1541.

Nuneaton (Warwickshire)
Where: Market Place, town centre
When: Saturday
What: vegetables, fruit, flowers, plants, garden shrubs and trees, garden ornaments. Perishable foods – fish, cheese, eggs, cakes, sweets, pet foods, cages and baskets etc, dress and curtain materials, wool, cottons, ribbons, lace, zips and trimmings, birthday cards, pottery, brass, wickerwork, jewellery, clothes, towels, bed-linens, shoes, boots, handbags, toys, lampshades, carpets, household cleaning equipment, saucepans, microwave ware

There are several pubs and coffee houses in Queens Road and the Market Place itself which serve lunch.

Oakham (Leicestershire)
Where: Market Place
When: Wednesday, Saturday
What: fruit, vegetables, fish, household goods, clothing, plants, and see below

Oakham used to be Rutland's county town, but in 1974 that county was merged with Leicestershire. People come from miles around to the twice-weekly provisions markets and to the Friday cattle market. Specialities in the food market are the fish stall on Wednesday, and pork pies on Saturday, which come from nearby Melton Mowbray and are particularly good. Pubs for lunch are the George Hotel in Market Place, the Crown Hotel in High Street, and the Rutland Angler in Mill Street.

Okehampton (Devon)
Where: Market Street
When: Saturday until 3 p.m.
What: fruit, vegetables, sweets, cakes, dairy produce, clothes, pictures, toys, cards, hardware, plants and shrubs, brassware

Okehampton is a market town in Dartmoor. Farmers travelling to it before dawn to sell their produce have to beware of invisible ponies, legendary black dogs and the ghost of Lady Mary Howard who journeys every night from Tavistock to Okehampton in a coach made from the bones of her murdered husbands, drawn by headless black dogs and driven by a headless coachman. Trading over, they can refresh their spirits at the White Hart Hotel or Plume of Feathers in Fore Street, or the Pretoria in North Street. The Cypriana, the Red Lion and the Coffee Pot in St James Street are also recommended. Okehampton holds a summer festival and sports week in July and a carnival in October.

Oldham (Greater Manchester)
Where: Tommyfield Market, on the corner of St Mary's Way and Lord Street (450 stalls) and in the Market Hall (70 stalls)

When: Monday, Friday, Saturday; a special antiques market on
Wednesday
What: fruit and produce stalls are open all week (half day Tuesday);
otherwise this is a general market

The Greaves Arms in Yorkshire Street is recommended for lunch.
There is a carnival in July and a summer show in August.

Oundle (Northamptonshire)
Where: Market Place
When: Thursday
What: fresh fish, fruit, vegetables, costume jewellery, clothes,
shoes, bags, plants, linen

Oundle market is very old, probably dating back to the twelfth
century. Market day was originally a Saturday and continued to be
so until about 1830, when Thursday took over. Between the wars
the market dwindled and almost disappeared, but it was revived
after World War II. The Angel in St Osyth's Lane and the
seventeenth-century Ship in West Street are two favourite pubs for
shoppers, and the Rose and Crown in Market Place and the Talbot
Hotel in New Street are also recommended. Oundle holds a feast
day on the Saturday nearest St Peter's day in New Street.

Ormskirk (Lancashire)
Where: Burscough Street
When: Thursday, Saturday
What: local vegetables, fruit, tinned goods, clothes, haberdashery,
cheese, gingerbread men

Sir Robert de Lathom secured a market charter in 1304 enabling
him to hold fairs at the Feast of St Barnabas, and markets every
Tuesday at his manors at Lathom and Roby. The connection
between Ormskirk and gingerbread dates back to the Crusades,

when a member of the Lathom family accompanied Richard the Lionheart to the Holy Land and brought back a liking for spicy foods. He had the local bakers experiment until they eventually produced a gingerbread to his liking. It is claimed that the same recipe is produced today. The land around Ormskirk was reclaimed from waterlogged moorland 200 years ago and since that time has become a rich vegetable-growing area.

A good pub for lunch is the Buck'ith Vine in Burscough Street, recommended for its reasonably priced food and delightful atmosphere.

Oxford

Where: Market Street
When: covered market, Monday to Saturday; open market, Wednesday
What: meat (including game), a large selection of fish, greengrocery, frozen foods, biscuits, sweets, snacks, fabrics (dress and furnishing), fashion, Indian fashion, hardware, household goods, wool, hosiery, underwear, watches, flowers, plants, bulbs, personality analysis, greetings cards, second-hand clothes, footwear, haberdashery, eggs, poultry, bric-à-brac, books, jewellery, gold and silver, washing-machine and vacuum-cleaner parts, luggage, handbags, leather goods, saddlery, lampshades, wholefoods, herbs and spices, dairy produce, Christian literature, sheepskins, china and glassware. The superb covered market also has video games, French bakery, cafés, a pizzeria, a pet shop and shoe-repairs

Oxford's annual fair, the St Giles Fair, takes place on the Monday and Tuesday after the first Sunday in September, except when 1 September falls on a Sunday, in which case the fair takes place on the Monday and Tuesday of the following week. Places to eat near the market are the Grapes, George Street; the Oxford Bakery and Brewhouse, Gloucester Street; and the Wheatsheaf, High Street. All offer live entertainment.

Pembroke (Dyfed)
There are two markets in Pembroke:

Pembroke Town Market, situated in Orchard Buildings, a cattle market, opens on Wednesday.
Pembroke Dock Market, a general market with produce and antiques, is situated in the Market Hall and opens on Friday.

The first charter was granted to the town in the second half of the twelfth century by Henry II, who confirmed certain 'customs' that had been allowed by his grandfather, Henry I, and added further concessions of his own, including the right to hold an eight-day fair and to have a guild of merchants. Today there is a funfair in the second week in October, which is organized by the Showmen's Guild of Great Britain.

The Railway Inn in Upper Lamphey Road serves lunch to shoppers in the town market; the Navy Inn in Fort Road is highly recommended for those in the dock market.

Penrith (Cumbria)
Where: Market Hall, Market Square
When: Tuesday, Saturday
What: vegetables, fruit, provisions, flowers, plants

Penrith is an old market town of red sandstone and the principal shopping area for the Eden district. The market is next to St Andrew's Church, which was established in 1133 although it was a site of worship long before that; the churchyard contains stones called the Giant's Grave and the Giant's Thumb, believed to date from 920. The market cross is an enclosed structure with a blue slate roof and a wooden frame, and serves as a bandstand when not on duty as a market. A maypole is erected here annually and forms the centrepiece of the May Day Carnival. The Two Lions is a nearby pub recommended for lunch.

Penzance (Cornwall)
Where: Causewayhead
When: Tuesday, Thursday, Saturday
What: small general market with about a dozen stalls

Near the market are the London Inn and Winston's Wine Bar. A livestock market on Tuesday at Long Rock sells cattle, sheep and pigs; and Penzance has an annual Corpus Christi Fair about eight weeks after Easter. The Penwith area is noted for its craft markets, and workshops making pottery, silver, enamelware, jewellery, leathercraft, woodwork and woolcraft are open to the public. Two in Penzance are the Barbican in Wharf Road and Cripples Ease Crafts, Nancledra.

Peterborough (Cambridgeshire)
Where: Market Place, Northminster
When: Tuesday, Wednesday, Friday, Saturday
What: high-quality locally grown fruit and vegetables, exotic herbs and spices, household goods, clothing, books, fish (brought daily from Grimsby), meat, poultry, plants

Peterborough market was first held under a charter of King Edgar dated 972. In 1876 the city council acquired the markets and fairs rights from the Church Commissioners and there have been regular weekly markets ever since. In June 1977 the £100,000, glass-fronted, fish and meat market was opened, followed two years later by the covered market. Places to eat nearby are the Bull Hotel, Westgate; Shelton's Store, Broadway; South China Seas, Midgate. In July Peterborough hosts the East of England Show and at the August Bank Holiday there is a festival of country music and Expo Steam.

Pickering (North Yorkshire)
Where: Market Place
When: Monday

What: clothes, shoes, fruit, vegetables, bacon, cheese, biscuits, cakes, fish, sweets, wool, plants, bulbs, materials, bedding, towels, household, leather goods, pet foods, bric-à-brac

The Black Swan at Birdgate is recommended for lunch: cock fights used to be held in this ancient inn. The White Swan and the Bay Horse are other good pubs in the Market Place. Pickering holds a carnival in early July, a traction engine rally in early August, and the Pickering Feast in September.

Pontypool (Gwent)
Where: Market Hall
When: Tuesday to Saturday
What: fish, fruit, vegetables, meat, flowers, plants, newspapers, periodicals, books, bric-à-brac, DIY equipment, clothes, footwear, jewellery, confectionery, wholefoods, snacks (40 stalls and as many casual hire tables)

In 1690 William and Mary granted the right to hold one weekly and three annual fairs in Pontypool. In 1730 Frances Bray, Lady of the Manor, built the Old Corn Market for trading in corn and other commodities, though this was certainly not Pontypool's first market. This market hall with its commemorative plaques still stands as a listed building – the ground floor is now a stationer's shop. In 1827 a rival market house was erected by William and Elizabeth Williams for the sale of butter and meat. As this infringed the market rights of the manor, Williams tried to buy them, but went bankrupt before he was able to do so. He was bought out in 1838 by John Griffiths, who also managed to purchase the market tolls. At this point the history of the market becomes confused, though it seems certain that someone succeeded in selling the market rights twice. Despite these wheelings and dealings, tolls had reverted to the lords and ladies of the manor by 1891, when they were sold yet again to the Pontypool Local Board.

Several pubs nearby provide appetizing, reasonably priced lunches (mainly sandwiches and grills) and excellent ale, and are clean and friendly with a good deal of local atmosphere, which is rightly prized above four-star furnishings. These are the Globe Hotel, Crane Street; the George Hotel and the Greyhound, Commercial Street; and the Winning Horse, Market Street.

Pontypool has an annual carnival on August Bank Holiday Saturday with fireworks, a funfair, children's entertainments, a motorcycle stunt show and an exhibition leading up to it.

Pontypridd (Mid Glamorgan)
Where: outdoor market in Market Square and Church Street; indoor market – access from Church Street and Taff Street
When: Wednesday, Saturday
What: fresh produce (meat, fruit, vegetables, dairy products) and textiles, clothes, china, cutlery, tools and carpets

In Christmas week Pontypridd market is open every day. Two pubs are specially recommended for lunch: Maltsters at Old Bridge and the Merlin Hotel at Pwllgwaun. These serve good food at reasonable prices, as do Princes Restaurant in Taff Street and John's Restaurant in Station Square.

Portsmouth (Hampshire)
Where: Charlotte Street
When: Thursday, Friday, Saturday
What: fruit, vegetables, meat, fish, gardening equipment, toys, bric-à-brac, plants, toiletries, cane furniture, materials

In the vicinity of the market there are Wimpy and other hamburger bars, and the department store Alders has a restaurant. The annual big event is the Southsea Show, held during the first weekend in August (including the Friday) on Southsea Common. There are equestrian events in addition to the main attractions, but these are held separately on the Thursday prior to the grand opening.

Port Talbot (West Glamorgan)
Where: covered market, Aberafon Centre shopping precinct; open market, town centre and behind Station Road
When: covered market Monday–Saturday (part early closing Wednesday); open market, Tuesday and Saturday
What: fish, meat, fruit, vegetables, clothes, household goods, shoes, bags, tinned goods (35 stalls)

One speciality of Port Talbot market is laver bread, a delicious edible seaweed that tastes like spinach and is often eaten with bacon and eggs at breakfast. The Aberafon shopping centre has two cafés, and the Old Vic is on the adjacent Riverside. In Station Road near the open market are St Oswalds and Ferrari's Café, and both serve lunch.

Preston (Lancashire)
Where: Market Hall, town centre
When: Monday, Wednesday, Friday, Saturday
What: vegetables, fruit, meat, dairy produce, fish, animal foods, a good selection of fabrics, clothing

Preston was first granted the right to hold a market by charter in 1179, and the Market Square or Flagged Market was its earliest known site. It was used right up until 1972, when the traders were moved to their present site in the covered market. Food traders operate from the adjacent Market Hall, erected in 1822 as a corn exchange. It now has 111 stalls, a café and a car-park. The Golden Cross is recommended for lunch because of its 'very good landlord'. Preston also has a cattle market, which was established on its present site in 1898 and is open for trading on Monday, Tuesday, Wednesday and Friday. The wholesale fruit and vegetable market in Bow Lane was opened in 1967.

Reading (Berkshire)
Reading has four main markets:

Where: Hosier Street
When: Wednesday, Friday, Saturday
What: fruit, vegetables, provisions, household goods, clothing

Where: Traders Indoor Arcade, 16–18 Station Road
When: Monday to Saturday
What: food, household, clothing

Where: The Emporium, Merchants Place
When: Monday to Saturday
What: antiques, junk and bric-à-brac

Where: Great Knollys Street
When: Monday
What: livestock

Great Knollys Street holds other sales during the week (information from the sale ground) and a horse sale on the first Friday of the month.

Redditch (Hereford and Worcester)
Where: Royal Square, adjacent to Kingfisher shopping centre
When: Tuesday, Wednesday, Thursday, Friday, Saturday
What: china, crockery, pictures, plants, shoes, ladies' and men's clothes, curtains, electrical goods, pet foods, bacon and sausages, toys, WI stall, health foods, freezer van, holiday firm, jewellery, handbags

The market was completely refurbished by the corporation in 1982–3. It is well organized and attractively laid out, with traditional coloured awnings over the open stalls.

Some of the major department stores in the Kingfisher shopping centre have restaurants serving lunch, or you could try Smiffs Wine Bar and Bistro, or the Grecian Kebab House. Redditch Carnival is held on the third Saturday in September, and features a procession of floats through the town centre, a funfair and side-stalls. The

Water Fiesta, held at the end of June at Arrow Valley Lake, offers a raft race, funfair and helicopter rides, besides many other attractions. Redditch Marathon is held on a Sunday in late August or early September and run over a course of more than 26 miles.

Retford (Nottinghamshire)
Where: The Square
When: general market, Thursday and Saturday; antiques market, Friday
What: the general market sells produce, clothing, household goods, plants and garden supplies. As well as antiques and bric-à-brac, the Friday market sells second-hand books and pictures

The most popular places to eat near the market are the White Hart, an old coaching inn with bar food and a restaurant, the Half Moon, and Sinclairs Restaurant and Coffee Rooms.

Richmond (North Yorkshire)
Where: Market Place
When: Thursday (in the Market Hall) and Saturday (outdoors)
What: produce, clothes, domestic goods and bric-à-brac, with an accent on woollen goods

Richmond is the market and meeting place of Swaledale. The cobbled Market Place lies in the shelter of the castle; the stalls are set up on Saturday as they have been for 900 years, and ancient halberds are placed outside the house of the mayor to show that he is the clerk of the market. In the days when the lead mines were worked, stockings knitted by all the members of the lead-miners' families were sold here. Richmond is still the place to buy sheepskins of all kinds and for knitters there are natural British wools, guaranteed pure to breed, from Wensleydale, Swaledale and Herdwick sheep. The twelfth-century Church of the Holy Trinity stands in the centre of the Market Place. There used to be shops inside the church but now it is a regimental museum: it continues its bell-ringing tradition, however. The Prentice bell is rung every day at 8 a.m. and the Curfew bell at 8 p.m. On Shrove Tuesday a Pancake bell is rung to remind people to make their pancakes.

The Bishop Blaize Hotel in the Market Square is probably the oldest inn in Richmond, and a good place for lunch.

Ringwood (Hampshire)
Where: Market Place
When: Wednesday
What: 'Anything from a cow to a clothes peg'

Ringwood is an attractive thirteenth-century New Forest market town particularly noted for its fishing in the River Avon. The town's market charter was granted by Henry III in 1226, and a special feature of the market is that the goods and produce on the stalls at the centre are sold by auction. The livestock market is nearby. Carnival day is the third Saturday of September. Trout is a local delicacy, and this can be sampled at one of the excellent restaurants around the market. In the Market Place itself are the Red Lion, the Original White Hart, and the Old Calcutta Restaurant, while a little further afield at Eastfield Lane is the Stuffed Trout.

Ripon (North Yorkshire)
Where: Market Place, city centre
When: Thursday
What: a wide variety of goods including food, household items, clothing, plants, flowers

Trading starts at 9 a.m., but in accordance with tradition the market is declared open by the ringing of a handbell at 11 a.m. On the Saturday before the first Monday of August each year, Ripon honours the Feast of St Wilfrid, the city's patron saint, with a procession through the town, the culmination of two weeks of merrymaking.

Rochdale (Greater Manchester)
Where: Market Street and Chapel Street
When: Friday, Saturday
What: fruit, vegetables, dairy produce, meat, fish, footwear,
haberdashery, clothes, general household goods. Muffins a
speciality; other local delicacies are cheese and chitterlings

There are several pubs and a number of fish-and-chip shops nearby,
and hamburger bars and cafés a short walk away in the town centre.
The local Rotary Club organizes a summer fair, and mummers'
plays are performed outside the parish church and in various pubs
on Good Friday. Rochdale also has an annual beer festival.

Rochester (Kent)
Where: Corporation Street
When: Friday, Saturday
What: a general market on Friday; a flea market with antiques,
second-hand clothes and bric-à-brac on Saturday

Rochester is proud of its connection with Charles Dickens and holds
a Dickens Festival in May/June, when more than a thousand people
dress up in Victorian costume. There is a Victorian cricket match, a
torchlight procession, a garden party and lots of street
entertainment including a 'Mr Rochester' competition. May also
sees the Rochester Chimney Sweeps' Procession and the Medway
Barge Race. In June there is the Admiral's Cruise: the mayor's
former jurisdiction over the river, from the Hawkwood Stone at
Burham to Sheerness, is recognized in a ceremony called 'the
Beating of the Bounds' up river to Hawkwood, then down river to
Garrison Point, Sheerness. In July is Admiralty Court: by a charter
of Henry VI in 1446 the bailiff of Rochester (and later the mayor)
became Admiral of the River Medway, and once a year the mayor
held court, with the aldermen and the jury of Free Fishermen,
afloat on the Medway to make laws for the regulation of the oyster
fishery and the taking of 'floating fish'. This ceremony is still
observed. The Admiralty Court sits in a barge moored at Rochester

Pier, the members having walked in procession in their regalia from the Guildhall. In July, too, there is the Medway Regatta, Carnival and Horse Show, followed by the Rochester Air Display in August.

Romford (Essex)
Where: General market and shopping hall, Market Square; North Street
When: Wednesday, Friday, Saturday
What: an extensive range of goods in the Market Square; antiques, second-hand goods and bric-à-brac in North Street

Romford has no charter, despite the size of its present market facilities: as the Royal Liberty of Havering, the market remained in the Crown's hands until its sale in 1829.

Romsey (Hampshire)
Where: Dolphin Hotel car-park
When: Friday, Saturday
What: fresh produce (meat, fish, vegetables, fruit, cakes, eggs, sweets), pet foods, clothes, children's clothes, antiques, second-hand furniture, jewellery

The White Horse Hotel in Market Place is a historic building (it was a medieval guildhall) and has the best bitter in town and good snacks at the bar. Romsey Show is held every second Saturday in September – it is a very popular country show with an average attendance of 24,000. Romsey Carnival is marked by a week of festivities in July/August. The Market Place is surrounded by quaint and attractive streets where the shopper can buy anything from a patchwork quilt to a herbal remedy or a piece of reject china. A visit can be combined with a tour of Romsey Abbey or the Mountbattens' home at Broadlands.

Ross-on-Wye (Hereford and Worcester)
Where: Market House
When: Thursday, Saturday
What: on Thursday there is produce, fish, some clothing, jewellery and plants; on Saturday the emphasis is on clothing, materials and miscellaneous goods rather than food

The first week in August sees Ross's annual carnival and there is a Biennial Festival of Arts at the end of May.

Rugby (Warwickshire)
Where: Gas Street, behind Church Street
When: Monday, Friday, Saturday
What: fresh produce, clothing, crockery, and see below

Rugby gave its name to Rugby football when William Webb Ellis, a pupil of Rugby School, carried the ball instead of kicking it in a soccer match in 1823. Rugby is proud of its traditions and the charter market boasts a Town Crier in a red coat, to be seen on Saturdays. An indoor market opens on Thursday as well as the other market days, and on Thursday, too, the WI holds a market in Brotherhood House, with refreshments available. Towards the station in Railway Terrace is Sheffields, the auction house, with auctions every Monday and the occasional antiques auction. The Mixed Spice Coffee Lounge in Castle Street offers cheap light lunches upstairs and a good view of the bustling street beneath. Peppers Coffee Shop in Sheep Street serves very good cheap wholefood and vegetarian dishes.

Saffron Walden (Essex)
Where: Market Place
When: Tuesday, Saturday
What: fruit, vegetables, tinned foods, meat, fish, fancy goods, clothes

Saffron Walden's central streets retain the layout they had in the Middle Ages and lie around the market, then as now the hub of this prosperous town. The market was transferred from nearby Newport in 1141 and by the thirteenth century, market traders were provided with permanent premises in Market Street and King Street. Between the fifteenth and the late eighteenth centuries the autumn-flowering *Crocus sativus* or saffron was grown around the town and formed a large part of its trade. It was used as a flavouring, an ingredient in perfume, and a medicine to treat catarrh, as well as a yellow dye for cloth. Expensive then as it is today, it made the town flourish and gave it its name.

There are plenty of places to eat round the market: the White Horse, Market Street; Upstairs Downstairs, Market Row; the King's Arms and the China Palace, Market Hill; and the Coffee House, Market Passage.

St Albans (Hertfordshire)
Where: St Peter's Street and Market Place
When: Wednesday, Saturday
What: general market

St Albans market dates back to 948, when Edred, grandson of Alfred the Great, granted permission for Ulsin, Abbot of St Albans, to hold, or perhaps replan, a market. It was held in an open triangle of land covering an area between Chequer Street, French Row and High Street. As the years went by permanent buildings were set up in place of the stalls. In 1539 St Albans was granted a charter by Edward VI, in which permission was given to the mayor and burgesses to hold a market every Wednesday and Saturday. A court was set up to deal with complaints of short-weight bread and weak beer – the offenders were fined and the proceeds were divided among the poor. A bell was rung at 10 o'clock to announce the beginning of trading. The market bell that was cast in 1729 was moved from the old market hall when this was demolished in 1855 and transferred to the clock tower, where it can still be seen. In the eighteenth and nineteenth centuries the Saturday market sold corn, eggs, poultry and butter. Wednesday was 'cow day', the cattle market day. Until the nineteenth century there were a number of ponds down St Peter's Street from which the cattle drank – Upper and Lower Cock Ponds, Monday's Pond and White Horse Pond – which were rented to householders and the proprietors of inns, who kept the banks and fences in good repair. Sadly, they have all been filled in. 1971 saw the last 'cow day', and two years later the Wednesday market, a smaller version of the Saturday market, was opened.

St Andrews (Fife)
Where: by the fountain in Market Street
When: Tuesday, Thursday
What: see below

Unfortunately there is no longer a set market day here as the old market has completely ground to a halt. But on Tuesdays and Thursdays a few people, but not more than two or three and not always the same people, erect tiny stalls by the fountain in Market Street. Sometimes it's someone selling flowers, sometimes cheap jewellery, and so on. Occasionally in the peak season a lady does weaving and spinning in the square by the fountain. On the second Monday and Tuesday in August is the Lammas Fair. This is a proper fair and market with stalls selling towels, linen, clothes, bags, jewellery, duvets, etc. There are no pubs close to the fountain, but towards the sea are hotels serving bar meals: the Ardgowan, Tudor, Niblick, Rusacks, Scores and St Andrews Golf.

St Austell (Cornwall)
Where: Market House, Market Street
When: every day; half-day Thursday
What: jewellery, sewing and knitting machines, poultry and dairy products, fruit and vegetables, confectionery, glass and chinaware, antiques, men's and boys' wear, household linen and bedding, boutique ladies' fashions, double-glazing, fresh fish, toys, hobbies and kits, charity gift shop, antique furniture, wool shop, leather

shop, café and snack bar, bookstall, fabrics and dress materials, stamps, coins, medals, records, floor coverings, outfitting, shoes, cycle shop for accessories and repairs, garden tools, hardware, DIY, small tools, camping equipment, pottery, stretch covers

The St Austell Market House is a remarkable building of great historical and architectural interest. The site of the building was previously the market-place, and records show that a small market building stood here in 1791. But the building was too small for a growing town and in 1842 Queen Victoria gave royal assent to an Act of Parliament which permitted the building of a new market house and town hall. It is a magnificent granite building – the stone was quarried locally and most of the cutting and shaping done on site by skilled masons. The blocks for the vaulted ceiling and the massive granite pillars in the entrance hall were cut by hand from detailed geometrical drawings and display superb craftsmanship. Stone stairways lead to the first floor, where a cast iron balustrade is set in granite blocks to form a gallery. The roof is unique, the great trusses being made of yellow pine with beams over fifty feet long.

To begin with, the market was open on Friday and Saturday for general trading, and on special occasions for exhibitions and fatstock markets. The centre of the ground floor was occupied by butchers' stalls, and the alcoves around the sides by live animals. The small room at the foot of the stairs, which now sells antiques, was the kitchen, where steaks and chops were fried all day and tea was served. On the first floor farmers' wives sold eggs, poultry, butter and home-made jam and cakes. The other balcony stalls offered fruit, vegetables, home-made sweets, peppermint rock, boots and shoes.

During World War I the meat market was closed and the Town Hall was converted into a cinema, with silent films and a piano. After the war, the market came back, and improved facilities for stallholders in the last twenty years have once again made it a thriving concern.

The Queen's Head and the Sun Inn, on either side of the building, have good pub food.

St Helens (Merseyside)
Where: Tontine Market, Lagrange Arcade; St Mary's Market, St Mary's Arcade
When: Monday to Saturday, except Thursday
What: both covered markets claim to sell 'just about everything except livestock': this includes fruit, vegetables, wickerwork, flowers, wool, pots and pans, and cheese

St Helens has a town show in July each year with stalls and amusements. Several pubs and eating establishments near the market serve food. Another nearby market is Earlstown market, Earlstown Market Square, Newton-le-Willows, Merseyside, which has traditional market stalls and is open on Friday.

St Ives (Cambridgeshire)
Where: Market Square
When: Thursday
What: general market, including produce, tools, clothes

St Neots (Cambridgeshire)
Where: Market Square
When: Thursday
What: fruit, vegetables, clothing, meat, fish, glassware, jewellery

St Neots was established by the Abbots of Bec in Normandy, after the Norman Conquest. The monks did much to build the place into a prosperous and active market town, which grew rich as a result of increasing river traffic along the Ouse, which has played an important part in the history of the town. The market rights were granted by Henry I at the beginning of the twelfth century. During the period of active river trade the buildings in the Market Square were occupied by merchants and the area surrounding it flourished – evidence of this is seen in the numerous public houses in the Square, which used to be lodging houses as well as taverns. River traffic disappeared from the town as a result of the Industrial

Revolution and with the advent of the railways, but St Neots market
still flourishes. The Square is believed to be the third largest market
square in England. St Neots has a carnival in the last week in August.

Salisbury (Wiltshire)
Where: Market Square, city centre
When: Tuesday, Saturday
What: fruit, vegetables, meat, fish, provisions, household goods

The market in Salisbury, or Old Sarum, as it was once known,
started in 1227 and is still open on the original market days. In 1865
the Salisbury Railway and Market House Company built the
Market House and a rail connection to Fisherton Station. Used for
many years for corn, cheese and wool, it was demolished in 1974 so
that the market could expand, but the magnificent façade was
preserved and now fronts the new library. Butcher Row and Fish
Row run along the south side of the market and to the north is Blue
Boar Row. There are several ancient half-timbered inns nearby,
notably the Haunch of Venison and the Rose and Crown on the
west side of the market and the House of John A'Port on the east.
An annual pleasure fair is held in the Market Square on the third
Monday of October.

Sandbach (Cheshire)
Where: main shopping centre
When: Thursday
What: one of the largest one-day markets in the North West, with
280 stalls and pavement stands spread round the Town Hall and
Market Hall

The market charter was granted to the Lord of the Manor, Sir John
Radcliffe, by Queen Elizabeth I on 4 April 1579. He also gained the
right to hold fairs at the Feast of the Virgin Mary in September and
during Easter week. The Manor of Sandbach had been in the
Radcliffe family for 250 years, but in 1611 he mortgaged and then

sold it; the rights were bought by Sir Randle Crewe and were passed down in the Crewe family until in 1889 Hungerford, Lord Crewe bestowed them as a gift on the town, together with the site for a new market hall, which is the one still in use today. An annual Elizabethan market is held to commemorate the charter every May Bank Holiday.

Sandwich (Kent)
Where: at the back of the Guildhall car-park
When: Thursday
What: a general market with a special auction of fruit, flowers and plants and a good WI stall with home-made preserves and cakes

Sandwich has been a market town since the sixteenth century when the River Stour silted up and put an end to its existence as one of Britain's Cinque Ports.

East Kent organizes a series of craft fairs throughout the year: for dates and venues contact East Kent Fairs, 201 London Road, Dover, or telephone (0304) 201644.

Sandy (Bedfordshire)
Where: Sandy free car-park (access from High Street or Cambridge Road)
When: Friday
What: fresh local produce, fruit and vegetables, clothes, footwear, meat, frozen food, plants, bulbs, shrubs, seeds, flowers

Many of Sandy's inhabitants commute to north Hertfordshire, Bedford or London, but those who don't are often involved in market gardening or farming, and the market is especially known for its locally grown vegetables. There are several fish-and-chip shops near the market, as well as pubs offering full or bar lunches: the King's Arms, London Road and the Bell, New Road are both very popular.

Saxmundham (Suffolk)
Where: Market Place, behind High Street
When: Wednesday
What: cheese, bacon, fruit and vegetables, plants and bulbs, clothes, towels, stretch covers, fish, sweets, and see below

On alternate Wednesdays Saxmundham has an antiques fair in the Parish Hall, and an auction of antiques, produce, etc takes place behind the opposite side of the High Street to the produce market.

Scunthorpe (Humberside)
Where: New Food Hall and Old Market Hall
When: the New Food Hall is open all week and the Old Market Hall trades on Friday and Saturday
What: a large range of general goods, excellent butchery stalls and fresh locally grown garden produce

The Pig and Whistle public house and Robert's Fish and Chip Café are nearby.

Selby (North Yorkshire)
Where: Market Place
When: Monday
What: general goods, produce

Selby market is busy, compact and attractive, and draws traders and customers from a thirty-mile radius. Special bus services run to Selby on Monday from all over West, South and North Yorkshire. Very large markets are held in Selby on Bank Holiday Mondays, when the town streets are closed to traffic and additional stalls are set up all over the town centre. A royal market charter was granted to Selby in 1304 by Henry de Lacy, Earl of Lincoln and Constable of Chester, who at that time held the Manor of Selby. Today the market is operated by Selby District Council. There are several pubs and hotels within easy range of the market.

Sevenoaks (Kent)
Where: Hitchen Hatch Lane; Bligh's Hotel; High Street
When: Wednesday (Hitchen Hatch), Friday (Bligh's Hotel),
Saturday (High Street)
What: goods on sale include produce, clothing, crafts and
bric-à-brac

The Farmers, opposite the Wednesday market, sells reasonably
priced home-made snacks and meals.

Sevenoaks has a summer fair with a street market, an open street
theatre and strolling players in late July. In the last week of June
and the first week of July there is the Sevenoaks Summer Festival,
at which the performing arts are celebrated.

Sheerness (Kent)
Where: Bridge Road in the town centre, opposite the bus and
railway stations
When: Tuesday throughout the year, and Sunday from mid-June to
the first week in September
What: the market concentrates on cheap summer clothes and there
is also a range of foodstuffs and household goods

The Railway Hotel with its 'Eastender' bar is nearest the market,
(which has been going for only a few years) or you can eat at the
True Briton in Cross Street. Sheerness has an annual carnival in late
July or early August.

Sheffield (South Yorkshire)
Sheffield has four markets:

Sheaf Market (Monday, Tuesday, Wednesday, Friday and
Saturday) sells food, mainly fruit and vegetables, and clothes, shoes
and fashion accessories, including bags and beads. It is particularly
good for leather jackets and shirts. The Garden, a pub serving food

at lunch-time and coffee throughout the day, is handy for the Sheaf Market, and for the next two markets, Castle and Setts.

Castle Market (Monday, Tuesday, Wednesday, Friday and Saturday) sells clothes, shoes, household goods, meat and fish. The fish stall is highly recommended.

Setts Market (Monday, Tuesday, Friday and Saturday) is an interesting place to browse for bric-à-brac as well as shoes, bags and some clothes. On Monday it is a collectors' and flea market.

The Moor Market (Tuesday, Wednesday, Friday and Saturday) sells fabric, clothes, shoes and small household goods. Hearty's, a restaurant in Wades furniture store, is a favourite eating-place for shoppers who like home cooking.

Sheffield has a Lord Mayor's Parade in June, the Sheffield Show in September, the Rag Week at the end of October, and the More the Merrier Week coinciding with the October half-term holidays.

Sherborne (Dorset)
Where: The Parade, Cheap Street
When: Thursday, Saturday
What: plants, fruit and vegetables, bric-à-brac, dairy products, health foods, wool, materials, second-hand books

This very attractive town offers plenty of temptation to the bargain hunter. It has seventeen antique shops, and holds an antiques and book fair monthly at Digby Hall, Hound Street. It is also a thriving craft centre, producing tapestries, individually designed knitwear, handspun and dyed wool, silks and cotton. The Sherborne silk mill, which dates from 1740, made silk for Queen Victoria's dresses. A craft market is held annually in October at Digby Hall and attracts craftsmen from much further afield than just Dorset. The Sherborne carnival is in August – profits go to charity. On the first Monday after 10 October is the Pack Monday Fair, ushered in at midnight on Sunday by Teddy Roe's Band. The whole of Cheap Street and part of South Street and Digby Road are closed to traffic for the day and stalls are set up offering a wide selection of goods.

In Cheap Street are the Greyhound and the Cross Keys Hotels.

Sheringham (Norfolk)
Where: Station Road car-park
When: Saturday
What: 'everything bar livestock'

Sheringham Carnival falls round the August Bank Holiday
weekend.

Shrewsbury (Shropshire)
Where: town centre
When: Wednesday, Friday, Saturday
What: fruit, vegetables, flowers, clothes, carpets, meat, poultry,
books, bread and cakes, household goods

Shrewsbury is at the centre of an agricultural area and has one of
the largest cattle markets in the country. It is famous for its flower
show, which has been held annually in August since 1875 apart from
short breaks during the two World Wars. There is a Youth Music
Week in July, a regatta and agricultural show in May, and the
British Isles Horse and Tractor Ploughing championships in
October. The Admiral Benbow is recommended for lunch because
of its atmosphere and good cheap bar food.

Sittingbourne (Kent)
Where: Bull Ground, Roman Square, off High Street
When: Friday
What: clothing, vegetables, fruit, meat, provisions

You can eat at the Bull or the Red Lion, and there are burger bars
in High Street and East Street. Sittingbourne Carnival is held in late
June.

Skipton (North Yorkshire)
Where: High Street
When: Monday, Wednesday, Friday, Saturday
What: knitware, fruit and vegetables, dairy products

In 1204, the Lords of Skipton (a corruption of 'Sheep-town') had fairs granted by King John every Saturday and on the feasts of St Martin and St James. Nowadays, festivities centre around the Skipton Gala on the second Saturday in June, when there is a parade through the town up to a fair in the park.

Apart from the High Street market, there are a number of stalls down the side of the Black Horse Hotel yard. Skipton is also noted for its livestock market, held on Mondays and Wednesdays.

Sleaford (Lincolnshire)
Where: Market Place, on East Gate
When: Monday
What: flowers, bulbs, potted plants, clothing of all types, carpets and rugs, bathroom mat sets, fruit and vegetables, jewellery and watches, curtains, curtain material, lightshades, blinds, kitchenware, glass, Pyrex, crockery, cutlery, confectionery, wool (sold on bobbins), pet foods, cards and gifts, wrapping paper, pictures, picture frames, small tools, small electrical goods, kitchen-cleaning ware, second-hand paperbacks, pastries and pies, fresh fish, cheese, bed-linen, health food, shoes

There are three places near the market offering a very reasonably priced lunch: these are the Lafford Restaurant, the Lion Hotel and the Rose and Crown public house. Every year in June Sleaford has a carnival with a procession of floats travelling through the town streets, followed by arena events which take place on the local recreation ground, surrounded by stalls set up by voluntary organizations as well as by local shops and businesses.

Southampton
Where: Kingsland Square, off St Mary's Street
When: Thursday, Friday, Saturday
What: fruit, vegetables, meat, fish, confectionery, clothes

This market has some very long-established stalls – Mr Underwood has been here for sixty years. The Plume of Feathers and the

Kingsland Tavern are close at hand. The Southampton Show is held in the first week of July each year.

Southend-on-Sea (Essex)
This popular holiday resort has three markets:

Where: Roots Hall market, Victoria Avenue
When: Thursday
What: clothes, toys, jewellery, household, furnishings, meat, vegetables, fruit, flowers
Nearby is Reids Public House and Wine Bar, recommended for its good food.

Where: Central Market, Elmer Approach, off High Street
When: Friday, Saturday
What: as Roots Hall (above)
The High Street has several fast-food restaurants and the nearest pub is the Dickens, Station Approach, which has bar snacks and a carvery.

Where: York Road covered market
When: Monday to Saturday
What: pet store, fabrics, shoes, clothes, jewellery, furnishings, meat, fruit, vegetables, second-hand books, records, babyware
A pub called Charlotte's in High Street is recommended for its food and pleasant surroundings.

Southend has a whole range of events catering for the holidaymaker, including the Easter sports festival, the multi-nation swimming gala in May, the vintage bus rally and raft race in June, the carnival and Thames barge match in August and the Old Leigh regatta and shopping festival in September.

South Molton (Devon)
Where: town centre
When: Thursday

What: vegetables, fruit, second-hand stalls, fish, handicrafts and home-made foods on WI stalls

Besides the covered Pannier Market in the town centre there is an open cattle market just outside the town. The Old English Fayre usually takes place in the second or third week in June.

Southwold (Suffolk)
Where: Market Place
When: Monday, Thursday
What: fruit, vegetables, plants, trinkets and bric-à-brac

The Victoria is a friendly pub with good bar snacks; there is also the Nelson, further down towards the sea, and the Crown, which is noted for its fine selection of wines.

Spalding (Lincolnshire)
Spalding has a cattle market in Swan Street on Tuesday and Saturday selling cattle, sheep, pigs, poultry and game. The Sheep Market, which sells general goods, not livestock, is open on the same days. This has 16 stalls. In the Market Place there are 74 stalls selling general goods. At the cattle market there is also an auction of wholesale produce (fruit, vegetables and flowers) and bulbs on Monday, Wednesday and Thursday from 1 p.m. to 4 p.m. On Friday the auction starts at 11 a.m. and bulbs only are sold.

  More than half Britain's bulbs are grown around Spalding and there is an annual Tulip Fair in May.

Stafford
Where: Market Hall – entrance in Market Square and Crabbery Street
When: Tuesday, Friday, Saturday
What: clothes, food, garden supplies, plants, crafts, toys, jewellery, books. Specialities are cheese and china

There has been a market in Stafford at least since the latter part of the twelfth century. By 1382 market day was established as Saturday. A Tuesday market was added in 1912 to sell local farm produce and the Friday market was started in 1955. By the fifteenth century the Market Place had a shambles and a cross. In the 1790s the Shire Hall was rebuilt to house the sections of the market dealing in eggs, cheese, poultry and vegetables; a new market hall was built in 1854 and was extended to house the butchers' market in 1880.

A further extension of the butchers' market in 1889 was used for the sale of fish, cheese, wool and crockery. A cattle market was held in Stafford from the fifteenth century until 1953, and up until 1877 there were also separate pig and sheep markets. Stafford has always of course had plenty of crockery to sell: in 1835 there was a special crockery market in Tipping Street known as the Pitcher Bank, but crockery was removed to the general market in 1927.

The Noah's Ark Inn in Crabbery Street was converted into a market office and refreshment room – sadly refreshments disappeared to make way for more offices in 1967, but the Nag's Head is nearby and recommended for lunch because it is a place of character.

The right to hold a fair on the eve of St Matthew was granted in 1261. By 1614 this had developed into a horse fair and later there were other fairs for cattle, pigs, hops, colts, wool, cheese, cheese and bacon, and sheep. In the latter nineteenth century animal fairs drew complaints from the residents about 'the disgusting filth and indecent scenes' they gave rise to, and in 1909 they were removed from smell and sight to Lammascote farm. But this venue proved too far from the station, and was ill equipped, and by the 1930s the fairs had petered out. Stafford now holds a biennial Arts Festival, the next being planned for June/July 1988.

Staines (Surrey)
Where: Market Square
When: Wednesday, Saturday
What: meat, vegetables, fruit, textiles, household goods

Staines market has been held here since 1218 and an annual May Fair was granted by Henry III in 1228 for the sale of horses, cattle and sheep. In the Old Market House, which no longer stands, Sir Walter Raleigh was committed for trial in 1603 for alleged complicity in a plot to put Arabella Stuart on the throne: the trial was held here because the Black Plague prevented courts from operating in London. The Blue Anchor Hotel in the Market Square is a fifteenth century building, with additions from 1721. Five of its windows were bricked up to avoid window tax, and they are painted with window frames and curtains.

Stamford (Lincolnshire)
Where: Broad Street, Ironmonger Street
When: Friday
What: clothes, vegetables, china, second-hand goods, curtains, hosiery, cane ware, plants, cheese, fish, flowers, fruit

A market was founded at Stamford nearly a thousand years ago. The original stone ford (from which the town's name derives) was built by the Romans across the river Welland. By the twelfth century, Stamford was a successful market town famous for its cloth, and in 1254 Henry III granted it a charter.

Stamford's infamous 'Bull Run', held on 13 November, was started by William, Earl of Warrenne in King John's reign, and continued until 1839. A bull was released and then chased by the townspeople, who intended to corner the animal with their clubs on the bridge. Often the bull jumped into the river in a vain effort to escape, but eventually it was slaughtered, the locals claiming that the meat was improved by the 'hunt'.

You can eat at the Model Fish Bar in Broad Street or the Coffee & Creme in Ironmonger Street.

Stevenage (Hertfordshire)
Where: indoor market, St George's Way, beneath the multi-storey car-park

When: Thursday, Friday, Saturday
What: food market, also plants, household goods, clothes, bedding, pet foods, footwear, sweets, cheese, meat

Stevenage Museum is right near the market and recommended for a visit. An annual charter fair is held in the High Street in September.

Stockport (Cheshire)
Where: Central Market Place
When: Tuesday, Friday, Saturday
What: a full range of goods including a wide selection of cheeses, and textiles

Stockport market is 700 years old and fine medieval houses enclose the Market Place. The Blue Boar is recommended as a friendly place to eat lunch, with a good mixture of people and reasonably priced plate meals and bar snacks. Stockport Carnival is held at midsummer.

In 1784 local farmer Jonathan Thatcher rode a cow from his farm to the market as a protest against the saddle tax imposed on horse-riding by George III. A cartoon of this famous event was drawn and displayed in the House of Commons.

Stockton (Cleveland)
Where: High Street
When: Wednesday, Saturday
What: an excellent variety of goods on 180 stalls

The original market charter was granted to Stockton by the Bishop of Durham, Bishop Bec, in 1310. The market cross was erected in 1768 and remains to this day. In 1770 Stockton held its first fair for horned cattle, sheep and horses as part of the open market in High Street; it was later transferred to a separate site now occupied by the Municipal Buildings. The Shambles was opened in 1825 and remained unaltered until 1985, when it was refurbished. The Corn

Market, next to the Shambles, closed in 1970. Spencer Hall Market replaced the Shambles as a building for butchers and food retailers in 1973. Pubs nearby are open all day, but try the Riverside for good food and quick service in excellent surroundings. Nearby there are other markets – at Thornaby town centre on Thursday and at Billingham town centre on Monday.

Stratford-upon-Avon (Warwickshire)
Where: Rother Street
When: Friday
What: fruit, vegetables, jewellery, wool, leatherwork, sweets, brasses, plants and gifts

The market in Stratford was founded by Charter of Edward VI on 28 June 1553. At about this time the Mop Fairs began; these are still held on 12 October (unless that falls on a Sunday) and the Runaway Mop (see page 12) on the Friday fortnight following that.

The Lamplighter, a pub in Rother Street close to the market, is owned by the town council, which takes special care to appoint a lessee with a very good reputation for the quality of the drinks and food he provides.

Stroud (Gloucestershire)
Where: Threadneedle Street and the Shambles
When: Friday (Threadneedle Street) and Saturday (the Shambles)
What: clothes, flowers, food, confectionery, crafts

Stroud is the home of fine cloth, including 'Stroud Scarlet', used in military uniforms. Both its markets are small and intimate. The Saturday market is on the site of the old meat market: two shambles tables, with knife and chopper marks, remain beneath the long early-nineteenth-century colonnade. John Wesley preached here, standing on a butcher's block. Opposite is the Town Hall with a rare oriel window from which civic dignitaries used to keep an eye on the market proceedings, and probably watched bull-baiting from a safe distance.

The Cotswold Coffee Lounge and the Swan Inn are both recommended for lunch. The Stroud Show is in July and the International Arts Festival in October.

Swadlincote (Derbyshire)
Where: town centre
When: Tuesday, Friday, Saturday
What: fruit, vegetables, clothes, crafts, shoes, leather goods, materials

The market is adjacent to the Delph, a pedestrian shopping-precinct which offers, in addition to a variety of eating places, regular Saturday entertainment – clowns, brass bands, magicians etc. Swadlincote also has a very lavish Christmas lights display from the end of November.

Swaffham (Norfolk)
Where: Market Place
When: Saturday
What: the open-air market sells general retail goods, but one corner is devoted to an auction sale of antiques

The market was established by charter in the thirteenth century. The week leading up to August Bank Holiday is Swaffham Carnival week. There are fifteen catering establishments round the market place – so there is a wide choice for lunch.

Swindon (Wiltshire)
Swindon has several markets:

Where: Brunel Centre
When: Monday to Saturday

Where: Fleet Street
When: Saturday, Sunday

Where: British Road Services Depot, Greenbridge
When: Wednesday to Saturday

Where: Blunsdon Abbey Stadium
When: Sunday (annual membership 30p)

All these markets have a wide variety of goods. In addition, on the last Thursday of each month there is an antiques market at the Planks Salerooms, and an auction is held there every Saturday, with viewing on Friday and before the sale on Saturday. The Salerooms open at 10.30 a.m.

Tamworth (Staffordshire)
Where: town centre – George Street, St Editha's Square, Lower Gungate Precinct, Market Street
When: Tuesday, Saturday
What: fresh provisions, household, textiles, clothes, pet foods, fish – a wide variety of goods on 140 stalls

Popular pubs near the market serving lunch are the Peel, Market Street, the Moat House, Lichfield Street and the Castle Hotel, Market Street.

Taunton (Somerset)
Where: Priory Bridge
When: Tuesday and Saturday
What: Tuesday, livestock; Saturday, livestock and clothes, material, cheese, butter, milk, meat, bacon

The history of Taunton market goes back beyond the Norman Conquest. The Domesday Book records a thriving market, but the town's royal charter dates from the reign of Edward the Elder, who ruled the Saxons from 901 to 925. Only Worcester is said to have a more ancient charter. Today's traffic-congested town centre, called the Parade, was originally an open space for the market. As temporary stalls became permanent, this area changed character and gradually filled up with shops, houses, inns and a market hall. Some of the original traders were pushed out – pig traders, for example, were forced to establish themselves in a separate pig market (hence Pig Market Lane) and stalls for carrots and cabbages moved to High Street. In 1772 some buildings were demolished to make way for the elegant Market House, designated by an amateur architect called Copleston Warre Bampfylde, which had flanking wings to shelter the remaining stallholders.

Apart from being a county town, Taunton serves the shopping, commercial and administrative needs of a large rural area. Places to eat near the market are the Crown and Septre (sic) and Market Kitchen Restaurant, which is opposite the market gates.

Taunton has an annual illuminated carnival procession on the third Saturday in October, preceded by the Taunton Cider Barrel Race. Barrel-rolling used to be a traditional pastime in many parts of the country – Taunton, centre of the cider country, is one of the very few places where this has survived. In the event, teams of two have to push firkins uphill for over half a mile (a firkin is the traditional name for a wooden cask that holds nine gallons of cider). The contestants wear either Somerset smocks and heavy boots or carnival costumes, and the prize is cash and a large quantity of cider. The procession afterwards occupies 1½ miles of road and the illuminated floats take an hour and a half to pass any given point. People flock to this carnival from all over the county.

Tenbury Wells (Hereford and Worcester)
Where: Round Market
When: Tuesday, Friday
What: linen, clothes, shoes, fish, greengrocery, confectionery, plants, and on Friday a WI stall with home produce

Tenby (Dyfed)
Where: High Street
When: Monday to Saturday
What: meat, greengrocery, pet store, dairy products, clothes, crockery, fish, travel agent, Welsh wool, tapestry

The Tenby Regatta is held in July and the Firemen's Carnival in August. The Normandie Hotel, close to the market, is recommended for its bar lunches.

Tewkesbury (Gloucestershire)
Where: town centre car-park
When: Wednesday, Saturday
What: a general market

The market does not have a charter, but there is a Mop Fair in October, when the streets are closed to traffic for a couple of days, and filled with sideshows and festivities.

Thame (Oxfordshire)
Where: Upper High Street car-park
When: Tuesday
What: fish, fruit and vegetables, bric-à-brac, records, clothes, health foods, pet foods, new books, cane furniture

There was already a prosperous market in Thame in Norman times and the official Royal charter was granted in 1215. By the fourteenth century permanent shop buildings, now Middle Row, had replaced the open market stalls. Middle Row has not been built on since. Thame has now passed its heyday as a market town, though the cattle market still ranks as third most important in the country.

   The great annual event is the Thame Agricultural Show, held on the third Thursday in September and reputed to be the largest one-day agricultural show in the country. For many years it has been held on the showground by Risborough Road, which has now become its permanent location. The Show fair, held in the evening and for the following two days, takes up the whole of the main street. The autumn Charter Fair held a few weeks later is much smaller, but it too takes up most of the main street.

The Black Horse in the Cornmarket is recommended for lunch. It is one of several old-established and very attractive hotels in Thame.

Tiverton (Devon)
Where: Market Hall, Market Place
When: Tuesday, Friday, Saturday
What: local fruit, vegetables and dairy produce, clothing and household items

There is a livestock market at Tiverton Junction, Willand on Wednesday, and Exmoor ponies are sold at Bampton Fair (seven miles from Tiverton) on the last Thursday in October. On the first Thursdays in June and October the mayor of Tiverton opens the Tiverton Fair at Coggan's Well in Fore Street. This spring provided the town with fresh water in the Middle Ages and still bubbles today. Recommended for lunch is the Half Moon, near the market.

Todmorden (West Yorkshire)
Where: adjacent to Market Hall and bus station
When: Wednesday, Friday, Saturday
What: food, clothing, jewellery, toiletries; also flea market on Thursday

Todmorden Carnival is held in May and the agricultural show in June. The Black Swan is immediately opposite the market and there are several cafés in the vicinity.

Tonbridge (Kent)
Where: Bank Street
When: Saturday
What: fruit, vegetables, clothes and household goods

There are several eating places in High Street close to the market.
The Tonbridge Festival is held every year in May.

Totnes (Devon)
Where: general market, High Street; Elizabethan Market, Civic
Forecourt
When: general market, Friday; Elizabethan Market, Tuesday
(summer only)
What: a wide variety of goods, and many hand-made items

According to local tradition, the town was founded by the
great-grandson of Aeneas, who named it 'Dodonesse' while
standing on the 'Brutus Stone', which still exists. An Anglo-Saxon
stronghold with its own mint before the Norman Conquest, it
became a Borough in the eleventh century. Under King John, it was
issued with a special charter of privileges, including the right to have
its own merchant guild.
   Totnes is also a town of Elizabethan heritage. On Tuesdays
during the summer, hand-made items can be bought at charity stalls
in the Civic Forecourt, where the vendors are dressed in full
Elizabethan costume.

Trowbridge (Wiltshire)
Where: Market Street
When: Tuesday, Friday, Saturday
What: fruit, vegetables, meat, fabrics, clothing, household goods,
fish

Trowbridge was a town that grew up with the woollen industry,
but today there is only one mill in operation. The market was originally held in the open air on the cobblestones in front of the fine

Georgian building now occupied by the Midland Bank. Here stood the town pump, round which the fish stalls were set up. Until about 1790 there was also an eight-sided covered market cross. It was taken down because it obstructed the traffic, and the stone ball that surmounted its roof can now be seen in the west porch of the parish church. The covered market hall was built in 1862 by a local woollen manufacturer, William Stancomb, and his lamb-and-flag crest can be seen on the gable. The façade has been restored and now leads to a covered shopping area. The stall market is in the basement of this precinct. The George Hotel in the old market place is a good spot for lunch.

Tunbridge Wells (Kent)
Where: Victoria Road
When: Wednesday
What: fruit, vegetables, fish, clothes, antiques (inside)

There is a weekly furniture auction in the Assembly Rooms in Lower Walk, and next door to this is a building that used to be the corn exchange – the statue above is Ceres, added in 1842. Fishmarket Square, which was used for that purpose in the nineteenth century, is now often filled with Morris dancers. The Pantiles, a broad walk at the heart of the town commissioned by Queen Anne, has many fascinating shops and restaurants and is particularly popular with antique collectors. In the summer it makes an ideal setting for street entertainers.

Tunbridge Wells, as the name suggests, grew up around its mineral springs which were discovered by Dudley, Lord North in the early seventeenth century. He claimed that the water cured him of 'a lingering consumptive disorder', and his recommendations brought a stream of aristocratic invalids to the area. In 1636 the locals responded by putting up two rest shelters next to the well, which later supplied visitors with coffee, writing materials and newspapers. In 1638 a raised tree-shaded walk was laid out and here local traders began to set up stalls selling fruit, vegetables, game and souvenirs. You can still take the waters at the entrance to the

Pantiles, though they are no longer credited with healing powers. The water has a metallic taste because it passes through the iron-bearing Hastings beds of the High Weald, though legend has it that the peculiar flavour has a more sinister origin: in the tenth century St Dunstan was said to have been tempted by a beautiful woman, and, realizing the danger he was in, took a pair of tongs out of the fire and seized her by the nose. The Devil immediately flew out of her and plunged his burning flesh into the spring, giving the water its distinctive metallic tang.

Wallingford (Oxfordshire)
Where: Market Place
When: Friday
What: fruit, vegetables, flowers, fish, haberdashery, fabrics, footwear, clothes

Wallingford is a market town and a resort for Thames boating. The WI holds a market in the Town Hall on Fridays, which sells flowers, eggs, cakes, home-made jams, and crafts. The Lamb Arcade is the antiques centre, formerly the Lamb coaching inn. The Michaelmas Fair is held on the weekend nearest 29–30 September. Places to eat are the Town Arms and the George Hotel, both in the High Street.

Wantage (Oxfordshire)
Where: Market Square
When: Wednesday, Saturday
What: fresh fruit and vegetables, eggs, fish, wholefoods, large selection of clothes, wickerware, cards, gifts, plants and shrubs, jewellery, carpets, sewing- and washing-machine spares, books

Wantage has been a market town since Roman times and a centre of milling, malting, wool, tanning and smithing trades. In addition to the market, three fairs are held each year in the Market Square, in May, September and October. There is also a summer carnival. The Vale and Downland Museum in Church Street is recommended for reasonably priced home-made food.

Wareham (Dorset)
Where: East Street
When: Thursday, and see below
What: Food, toys, crafts and clothing, with some seasonal variation,
and see below

Wareham also has a fortnightly furniture auction in the market
rooms on Tuesdays, which is very popular. This sometimes includes
chandlery and/or antiques and jewellery. There are seven
pubs/hotels within walking distance of the market and each one is
very different in character from the others. Wareham's annual
events are a town carnival, folk festival, the Purbeck Show and the
Cuckoo Fair.

Warrington (Cheshire)
Where: Bank Street
When: Monday to Saturday
What: fresh produce, fish, textiles, household goods clothes, plants
(256 stalls)

Warrington's market charter was granted in 1255 when the town
had a mere 700 inhabitants. It enabled it, though so small, to
establish a trading supremacy in this part of the country which has
increased over the centuries. In 1285 the trading facilities of the
charter were expanded by Edward I and the markets and fairs
attracted linen from Ireland, broad and narrow cloths from
Yorkshire, as well as horses, cows, sheep, goats, swine, and animal
pelts, fleeces, hides and skin. Because of the prosperity of its
market, Warrington made a good recovery from the pestilence and
famine that followed the Civil Wars in this area – in 1673 it was
described as 'a very fine and large town, which hath a considerable
market for linen, cloth, corn, cattle, provisions and fish, being
resorted to by the Welshmen, and is of note for its lampreys'. A
hundred years later the market was again praised for its fish – it is
interesting to note what came out of the Mersey and the sea just
beyond in the late eighteenth century – not only lampreys, but

sturgeon, greenbacks, mullet, eels, lobsters, shrimp, prawns, and the best and largest cockles in all England.

The market rights belonged to the Barons of Warrington and later the Lords of the Manor until 1851 when the newly formed Corporation bought them and started construction of a market hall shortly afterwards. They also made provision for privately owned markets in the immediate area, and these have given their names to Horsemarket Street, Buttermarket Street and Pig Hill. The new Warrington Market is a visually striking building that was opened in 1974. A pub has been built adjacent to it.

Warwick
Where: Market Place
When: Saturday
What: fruit, vegetables, provisions, clothes, household goods

Warwick's Market Hall was built in 1670 and today it houses the town's museum. Its arches provided a covered space for stalls until the nineteenth century, when they were railed off and used for the stocks. Right up to 1872 drunkards were punished by having to pull the stocks, which were on wheels, under the arches and then being locked in them. In the Market Place itself are the Bar Roussel, Giuseppe's, the Woolpack Hotel and the Jolshah Tandoori.

The Mop Fair dates from the reign of Edward IV (1461–83) and takes place on the Saturday nearest 12 October. It is opened by the mayor, who reads the charter at 12 noon. An ox or hogs are roasted in the car-park of the Globe Hotel, the mayor auctioning the first slice in aid of charity. The Runaway Mop (see page 12) is held on the following Saturday.

In the first week of December the Chamber of Trade organizes a Victorian Evening, when shops stay open late to offer their customers traditional Christmas fare, shopkeepers and customers dress in Victorian clothes, and penny-farthings are to be seen in the streets.

Wellingborough (Northamptonshire)
Where: Market Place, Market Street
When: Wednesday, Friday, Saturday. The market is let to a private operator, Countrywide Markets Ltd, for a bric-à-brac market on Tuesday
What: 166 stalls sell a wide variety of goods

The Golden Lion in Sheep Street is a handy pub with reasonably priced food.

Wells (Somerset)
Where: Market Place
When: Wednesday, Saturday
What: clothes, produce, fancy goods, fish, meat etc

Wells Market Place features an unusual grotto-style fountain, erected in 1799 to replace the medieval conduit which had supplied the market with water. On the north side of the Market Place is a row of stone buildings with bay windows, built by Bishop Thomas Beckington in the fifteenth century: you can still see a few butresses and half of one medieval window. Inside, most of them still have their original fifteenth century ceilings. On the south side of the Market Place is the Crown Inn, a fine timber-framed coaching inn displaying many seventeenth-century characteristics. From one of its upper windows the Quaker William Penn started to preach in 1695, but was arrested before he could finish. In the sixteenth century a market hall stood in the middle of the Market Place, open at the ground floor, with chambers above. This was demolished and the present Town Hall on the south side of the Market Place erected in 1779. Like the previous building it housed market stalls in its open ground floor and court rooms and assembly rooms behind and above. In the nineteenth century the ground floor was enclosed and a new covered market was built – this has since been converted and is now the post office on the east side of the Market Place. Also on the east side are two tall medieval gateways, built by Bishop Beckington. One is called the Bishop's Eye and leads to a leafy

green – a lovely spot in summer to sit and rest or picnic. The other is
called the Penniless Porch, because beggars used to shelter there,
waiting for kind church-goers to take pity on them.

Whitby (North Yorkshire)
Where: Market Square, Church Street
When: Saturday
What: fruit, vegetables, clothing, bric-à-brac, plants, fish, jewellery

Whitby is a fishing town, the home of Captain Cook and the
Endeavour, and famous for its Abbey founded in 657 by St Hilda, as
well as for appearing in three chapters of Bram Stoker's novel
Dracula (1897). It has a lovely old arcaded and roofed stone
market-place. Apart from fish, another local speciality much sought
after by shoppers is jet, a form of fossilized wood found on the
beach and made into jewellery by local craftspeople. Whitby
harbour nearby is bursting with likely eating-places catering for its
holidaymakers – fish and chips a speciality.

Wilton (Wiltshire)
Where: Market Place
When: Thursday
What: food, china and antiques, clothing and general goods

The right to hold a market in Wilton was first granted by charter of
Henry I dating from 1133. It is the oldest surviving charter in the
country and reads (in a rather awkward translation):

> Henry King of the English to his justices, and his sheriffs and his
> ministers, and his faithful subjects of all England, and the ports of
> the sea, greeting.
> I commend that my burgesses of Wilton of the Merchants
> Guild and of my customs of Wilton may have all the immunities
> and liberties of toll and passage, and all their customs, as well and
> as freely as my burgesses of London and Winchester better and
> more freely possess.

And if anyone unjustly interfere in this behalf, the penalty of ten pounds.

By 1361 there was a good deal of friction between the people of Wilton and Salisbury, whose markets were only some three miles apart. Wilton people took to stopping traders on their way to Salisbury and forcing them to set up stalls at Wilton market. Eventually it was decided that Wilton should hold its market on Monday, Wednesday and Friday, while Salisbury held its on Tuesday, Thursday and Saturday. The Wilton market gradually fell into disuse as the prominence of Salisbury increased, but in 1980 Salisbury District Council revived the Wilton market, fixing its opening day as Thursday.

A pleasure fair in mid-October, just before Salisbury Fair, takes place in the Market Place. There are three Sheep Fairs, held in August, September and October on the second Thursday in the month, the August Sheep Fair being the successor to the former Britford Fair (Britford is three miles south of Salisbury). The September Fair is the main one, and is held by virtue of a charter granted by Henry VI in 1433. It is claimed to be the largest in south-west England, with 120,000 sheep sold each year.

You can lunch in the Market Place at the Greyhound Inn, or in Minster Street at the Pembroke Arms.

Wimborne Minster (Dorset)
Where: Market Place
When: Friday (till 2.30 p.m.) Saturday (till 1 p.m.), Sunday (till 4 p.m.)
What: a large general market which includes an antiques bazaar on Friday

The market was established about 120 years ago and the antiques bazaar is a popular venue for collectors. There are several old inns and hotels in the square beneath the Minster. The Wimborne Minster Arts Festival is held in alternate years at the end of June and beginning of July, and the Wimborne Folk Festival takes place every year around 10 June.

Winchester (Hampshire)
Where: Middlebrook Street car-park
When: Wednesday, Friday, Saturday
What: fruit, vegetables, flowers, fish, cheese, health foods, pet
foods, clothes, bric-à-brac

St Giles' Fair has been held in Winchester since the twelfth century.
It was originally organized by the bishops to raise funds for the
cathedral, which took 300 years to build and was completed in
about 1300. Today the September fair raises money for clubs and
charities.

The Royal Oak is the oldest pub in Winchester, and this is
recommended for lunch, together with the Baker's Arms, which is
noted for always being full of flowers. The Box Tree is also close to
the market and has tables outside.

Windsor (Berkshire)
Where: Sun Passage, access from Victoria Street
When: Saturday
What: various, including ladies' clothes, fruit and vegetables, meat,
toiletries, eggs and cheese

There are about twenty traders in this market, though it is hoped
that their numbers will soon be swelled to around fifty. Some
traders' families have been established here since the early years of
this century. The market dates back to a charter of James I, part of
which reads: '. . . and also we will and by these present grant for
our heirs and our successors to the aforesaid mayor, bailiffs and
burgesses of the aforesaid town and their successors for ever that
they themselves and their successors shall have, shall hold and shall
keep, and they shall have power to and shall be able to have, hold
and keep a market in the aforesaid town every year for ever in this
way weekly on a Saturday.' And so it has been since 26 August
1603.

Under the statue of Sir Christopher Wren, right by the Castle, a
couple of stalls selling goods, sometimes for charity, are also in

action on a Saturday. There are plenty of eating places near the market in Peascod Street.

Winsford (Cheshire)
Where: town centre
When: Thursday, Saturday
What: a variety of stalls, specialities being vegetables and cheese

The Queen's Hotel is recommended for lunch. The Tour of Winsford Half Marathon is held on Easter Sunday to raise money for the mayor's charity, and there is an autumn carnival and fair.

Wisbech (Cambridgeshire)
Where: Market Place, town centre
When: Thursday, Saturday
What: fruit, vegetables, fish, clothes, bric-à-brac, plants, flowers

Wisbech has a mart fair early in March and a statute fair at the end of September. The Rose and Crown in the High Street is recommended for lunch.

Witney (Oxfordshire)
Where: Market Square
When: Thursday, Saturday
What: fruit, vegetables, fish (Thursday only), cakes, plants and flowers, antiques, pet foods, cards, brassware, all sorts of clothing, shoes, cheese, basketware, bric-à-brac, Hoover parts, books, bedding, linen, materials, cane work, confectionery, second-hand prints, pottery, foam

Witney has been a market town producing woollen cloth and blankets since the thirteenth century. Blanket Hall in the High Street was built in the eighteenth century by the Witney Blanket Weavers Company for the weighing and measuring of their blankets. In Market Square is the Buttercross, which has been the meeting place for local traders since the Middle Ages. The clock tower on top of it was added in 1683.

The Witney Feast is held every September on the Leys Recreation Ground, and there are four pubs close to the market: the Cross Keys, the Marlborough (which is specially recommended), the Angel and the Fleece.

Woodbridge (Suffolk)
Where: Market Hill
When: Thursday
What: fruit, vegetables, health foods, fish, bric-à-brac, clothing, wool

Worcester
Where: The Shambles (indoors) and Cornmarket (outdoors)
When: indoor market, Monday to Saturday; outdoor market, Friday and Saturday
What: vegetables, fruit, household goods, meat, fish, cheese, eggs, bric-à-brac, flowers

Worcester is the birthplace of the composer Elgar and once every three years it hosts the Three Choirs Festival in August, which revolves between Hereford, Worcester and Gloucester. It is also the home of the Worcester Royal Porcelain Company, founded by Dr John Wall in 1751, and the factory and museum in Severn Street are open to visitors. The antique shops in Friar Street and around Sidbury are an irresistible attraction to collectors and bargain hunters. Worcester is also known around the world for its sauce, which has been made at the Lea & Perrins factory in Midland Road since 1850.

Worthing (West Sussex)
Where: Richmond Road
When: Saturday

What: fruit, vegetables, fish, meat, clothes, household, eggs, flowers

The Wheatsheaf is next to the market and serves lunches. In July Worthing holds a Seafront Fayre and Market, three days of informal entertainment along the promenade with a market on the Saturday evening.

Wymondham (Norfolk)
Where: Market Place, Market Street
When: Friday
What: vegetables, fruit, fish, meat, bread, clothing, sweets, plants

The picturesque Market Cross dominates Wymondham Market Hill. It was erected in about 1618 on the site of an earlier structure which had been built in 1286 but was destroyed in the great fire of 1615, as were many of Wymondham's medieval buildings. One of the few remaining is the fourteenth-century Green Dragon in Church Street, which is recommended for lunch. The market cross is a half-timbered octagonal building resting on wooden pillars with stone bases. The pillars and beams are carved with representations of tops, spindles, spoons and skewers, emblems of wood-turnery, the staple industry of the town. On Friday in the area behind the market cross there gathers a small but colourful market. This practice has only recently been revived, though the rights of market were granted to the town by King Henry in 1440.

Yeovil (Somerset)
Where: Petters Way
When: Friday
What: fresh produce, clothing, household goods, plants

Local pottery, saddlery, antiques, home-made cider and silk from Britain's only silk farm – Lullingstone Silk Farm, Compton House, near Sherborne – are some of the reasons for visiting the Yeovil

district. Yeovil Carnival is usually held in November and is one of
the Somerset Light Carnivals with spectacularly illuminated floats
put together with tremendous skill and patience. Yeovil's prosperity
was built on glove-making and leatherware, and the town is still an
important centre for sheepskin goods of all kinds.

York
Where: Newgate
When: Monday to Saturday
What: fresh fish, fruit and vegetables, clothes, textiles (furnishing
and dress fabrics), household goods, bric-à-brac

York is an important centre for trade in antiques, silver, jewellery
and furniture, and the Department of Tourism, de Grey House,
Exhibition Square can supply free of charge details of the various
specialist fairs held in the city throughout the year. These include
regular fairs of antiques, crafts, records and stamps.

The Bari Restaurant in The Shambles, the old butchers' quarter
adjoining the market, serves good Italian food.